ETHNIC CHRONOLOGY SERIES
NUMBER 15

The Japanese in America

1843-1973

A Chronology & Fact Book

Compiled and edited by

Masako Herman

1974
OCEANA PUBLICATIONS, INC.
DOBBS FERRY, NEW YORK

To Ken, Ellyn, and Amy

Library of Congress Cataloging in Publication Data

Herman, Masako, 1930-   comp.
    The Japanese in America, 1843-1973.

    (Ethnic chronology series, no. 15)
    Bibliography: p.
    1. Japanese in the United States -- History. I. Ti-
tle. II. Series.
E184.J3H46   917.3'06'956   74-13106
ISBN 0-379-00512-3

Manufactured in the United States of America

TABLE OF CONTENTS

APPENDICES

EDITOR'S FOREWORD

The history of the Japanese in America has been relatively short and for those on the West Coast, especially in California, it was fraught with hardships and frustrations. Yet despite many obstacles it has generally been a success story. Whether the success can be attributed to an ethnic cohesiveness due to a hostile environment, to an inherent teaching of pride in their philosophy, to a spirit of competitiveness, or to a desire to be accepted is but for psychologists and social scientists to ponder.

Unlike some of the other minority groups of the country, the mother country had always played a role in the life of the Japanese in America. For instance, when there had been excessive anti-Japanese sentiment exhibited against the Japanese in California, there would follow a dialogue between the governments of Japan and the United States. On other occasions the activities of Japan have brought reactions by the larger majority of the white population upon the Japanese residents of the United States. These occurrences have been used as a political lever at times by bother governments.

The valiant deeds of the Nisei men of the 442nd Infantry Regimental Combat Team, the lawful cooperation by over 100,000 Japanese of the West Coast when they were incarcerated in ten "concentration" camps during World War II, the varied role in which the JACL performed, and the many personal efforts and sacrifices of others are but a few examples that demonstrated the spirit of Americanism of the Japanese people. This same spirit underlies their continued participation in more expanded fields of endeavor and has been undeniably instrumental in contributing to the larger fabric of the history of America in its democratic principle.

The author feels gratitude and indebtedness in having had the opportunity to compile this outline history of the Japanese in America for in so doing she learned history from a new perspective. The experience was eye-opening as well as enriching. It is the author's hope that this book, which does not purport to be complete by any means, will be able to stimulate its readers to further studies and that these in turn may serve to bridge the gaps in those history books where omissions have been made.

Acknowledgement and gratitude are extended to those who actively assisted the author, each in their own unique way: Sherie Chalakani, William H. Fanning, Jr., Bill Hosokawa, Sally Joseph, Jean Kariya, and Rae Okada; also to those who generously contributed research material: Shig Kariya, Austin P. Magner, Aki Shirai, Ippei Shimizu, Leslie Susser, Edison Uno, Ron and Miye Yoshida, and George Yuzawa.

1843   May 7. Manjiro Nakahama, also known as John Mung, was rescued at sea by Captain William H. Whitfield of the whaler John Howland and was brought to New Bedford, Massachusetts. Nakahama is given credit as being the first Japanese in America.

1850   Hikozaemon, also known as Hikozo Hamada and Joseph Heco, was rescued at sea by the American sailing ship Auckland. He was taken to San Francisco; then he studied in Baltimore and became the first Japanese naturalized citizen.

1853   July 8. U.S. Commodore Matthew Calbraith Perry anchored at Edo Bay and attempted to "open the door" to Japan.

1854   March 31. Treaty of Kanagawa formalized relations between America and Japan.

1858   July 29. Townsend Harris, American consul general, negotiated a full commercial treaty with Japan (the Edo Treaty), which had been initiated two years earlier.

1860   March 17. Kanrin Maru, an escort corvette to the U.S.S. Powhattan, arrived in San Francisco. Among those aboard was Manjiro Nakahama, who had been the first Japanese in the United States, as special officer and interpreter.

March 29. The frigate U.S.S. Powhattan arrived in San Francisco with the Japanese Grand Embassy aboard, headed by Masaaki Shimmi, Buzen-no-Kami.

April 7. The Japanese Grand Embassy left San Francisco on the U.S.S. Powhattan for Washington, D.C. by way of Panama to Apsinwall on the Gulf of Mexico, then boarded another frigate, the U.S.S. Roanoke, to Hampton Roads, Virginia, where they were transferred to a river boat which took the Potomac to Washington, D.C.

May 17. The Japanese delegation presented the Shogun's (the then head of Japan) letter to President James Buchanan.

May 22. Documents pertaining to the Treaty of Amity and Commerce were exchanged between the United States government and the Japanese Grand Embassy.

November 9. The Japanese delegation returned to Yokohama, Japan, on the U.S.S. Niagara.

1864	Jo Niijima, also known as Joseph Hardy Neesima, arrived in America as a stowaway. The ship's owner, Alphaeus Hardy, sent him to Phillips Andover Academy and Amherst College.
1866	Two samurai (warlords) were sent by Japan to study at Rutgers University.
1867	Yukichi Fukuzawa visited America for the third time. An educator and author, he was instrumental in educating feudal Japan about the Western world.
1868	June 19. The first emigration to Hawaii consisted of 148 Japanese contract laborers. Upon learning of mistreatments of her people by the plantation owners, Japan halted emigration.
1869	May 27. The first group of immigrants to arrive in the United States settled in Gold Hill, California, and set up the Wakamatsu Tea and Silk Farm Colony.
1870	Joseph Hardy Neesima graduated from Amherst College and entered Andover Theological Seminary.

Manjiro Nakahama accompanied another mission from Japan on its way to Europe. He paid a brief visit to his benefactor, Captain William H. Whitfield, in Fairhaven, Massachusetts

Tanetaro Megata attended prep school, entered Harvard and eventually graduated with a law degree.

About this time, twelve students from Japan were admitted to Annapolis Naval Academy by special Congressional permission. Other students were to be found at Harvard, Yale, Princeton, Cornell, and New York Polytechnic Institute. |
| 1872 | Iwakura Mission, comprised of fifty-four students, visited Boston. Neesima was the interpreter who accompanied them to Europe and he returned to complete his education at Andover Theological Seminary.

Kentaro Kaneko, one of the students of the Iwakura Mission, went to Harvard and studied law under Oliver Wendell Holmes. He was a classmate of Theodore Roosevelt.

Tadaatsu Matsudaira arrived in America, attended Rutgers University, and received a civil engineering degree. |

1875   Kanaye Nagasawa arrived in Santa Rosa, California. He helped Thomas Lake Harris, a humanitarian, to found New Life, a Christian order, on 2,000 acres of land called Fountaingrove.

1876   Japan participated in the Centennial Exhibition in Philadelphia by erecting a typical Japanese house.

     Around this time, Yamanaka & Co. established branch stores in New York and Boston.

1879   The Japanese Gospel Society, headed by Kanichi Miyama, was formed in San Francisco.

1880   Between 1871 and 1880, the U.S. Bureau of Census reported 149 Japanese immigrants to mainland U.S.A.

     Around this time, the branch offices of the Yokohama Specie Bank opened in New York and San Francisco.

1885   February 8. Japan signed a treaty with Hawaii that again allowed contract laborers to leave Japan. The ship, City of Tokio, arrived with 859 laborers, women, and children.

1886   Japan legalized emigration, which had been suspended in 1868 due to mistreatment of her people by the Hawaiian plantation owners.

     Tadaatsu Matsudaira was appointed Colorado's Assistant Inspector of Mines. He married the daughter of Archibald Sampson, a retired general of the U.S. Army.

     Hachiro Onuki, also known as Hutchlon Ohnick, was granted a franchise to supply gas and electricity to Phoenix, Arizona. He had two partners named W.C. Parsons and Josiah White.

1887   Kikumatsu Togasaki arrived in the United States and became a pioneer merchant. He founded the Mutual Supply Co. in San Francisco to bypass the boycott of Japanese laundry operators by the wholesale houses.

1888   Tadaatsu Matsudaira, first Japanese resident of Colorado, died.

     Several Japanese entered Vaca Valley, California, as farm laborers.

1889   Kinji Ushijima, also known as George Shima, arrived in the
            United States. He gained the backing of an American firm
            that owned some delta land along the San Joaquin River and
            proceeded to convert this swamp land to usable land for po-
            tatoes. Shima became so successful he was known as the
            "Potato King."

            Iwao Yoshikawa applied for naturalization and obtained his
            first papers.

            The Japanese Methodist Church was founded in Oakland,
            California.

1890   Masajiro Furuya arrived in Seattle, Washington, and opened
            a tailor shop. In time he became a banker, merchant, and
            manufacturer.

1891   Shiro Fujioka arrived in the United States. He was the ed-
            itor for North American Times, Seattle, Washington, a
            writer for Rafu Shimpo, Los Angeles, California, president
            of the Central Japanese Association of Southern California,
            and chairman of the Rice Campaign, which sent rice to the
            hungry people of Europe.

1892   The Japanese Baptist Church opened an English night school
            in San Francisco.

1893   San Francisco Board of Education Director Burke introduced
            a resolution providing a segregated Chinese school for all
            Japanese children. Japanese Consul Sutemi Chinda protested
            Burke's resolution. After receiving Consul Chinda's protest,
            the Board of Education voted to rescind the resolution.

            Japan erected a pavilion at the World's Fair in Chicago.

1897   Hawaii signed a treaty with Washington, D.C.

1898   Hawaii was annexed as a territory. This enabled the 60,000
            Japanese already in Hawaii to proceed to the United States
            without passports if they so desired.

            Kyutaro Abiko bought and merged two Japanese newspaper
            businesses and created the Nichi Bei Times in San Francisco
            with four friends. He also organized the California Land
            Co., which established the Yamato Colony and settled many
            Japanese immigrants near Livingston, California.

Manjiro Nakahama, the first Japanese in America, who taught navigation and engineering at Japan's Naval Training School, served as interpreter, and did much to bridge the initial gap between Japan and America, died in Japan.

Seven Japanese crewmen died in the sinking of the U.S. battleship <u>Maine</u> in Havana harbor, which touched off the Spanish-American War.

May 1. Other Japanese served the U.S. Navy in the Battle of Manila Bay.

1899 In this year, 2,844 Japanese entered mainland United States from Hawaii.

September 2. Two Buddhist priests arrived in America. Their arrival is regarded as the founding date for the Buddhist Churches of America.

1900 The Japanese Association of America was founded in San Francisco to fight racial discrimination.

Harry Yaemon Minami began shipping vegetables from California to all parts of the country.

Jutaro Nakata arrived in the United States and converted a piece of California's barren land into a rich vineyard. He became director of the Industrial Bank of Fresno and was a trustee of the Church of Bowles.

In this year, 12,635 Japanese from Hawaii entered the United States, causing alarm in the West.

Zintaro Yamada arrived in California. He was the first to introduce a modern system in truck gardening. Yamada served for three successive terms as president of the Japanese Farmers' Association.

March. Mayor James D. Phelan of San Francisco ordered mass inoculation of the Japanese and the Chinese -- but no others -- in a false bubonic plague scare.

April 30. The Organic Act was signed by President McKinley; it set up the territorial government of Hawaii.

June 14. Hawaii was incorporated as a territory of the United States.

August. The Japanese government announced the denial of further passports to laborers for mainland United States but declined to mention Hawaii. This was the first Gentleman's Agreement.

1901   Hachiro Onuki (Hutchlon Ohnick) went to Seattle, Washington, and opened the Oriental American Bank with two other Issei (a term for a Japanese born in Japan).

Dr. Jokichi Takamine, a chemist, isolated pure adrenaline and made the formal announcement by presenting his paper at Johns Hopkins University. Takamine also discovered an enzyme that broke down carbohydrates and called it Takadiastase, which Parke Davis Pharmaceutical Co. began producing commercially. Through the years he had been involved in various industries such as fertilizer, distillery and printing, both in Japan and in the United States.

1902   Saibara Saito was asked by the Japanese government to study rice-growing potential in Texas while he was studying theology at Hartford, Connecticut. He settled in Webster, Texas, and harvested his first rice crop two years later.

October 8. Saburo Kido was born in Hilo, Hawaii.

1903   Kinzo Yasahara came to America and started a hotel and brewery business in Los Angeles. Due to Prohibition, he converted the brewery to a miso (soy bean paste used for soup) and soy sauce factory. Yasahara also supplied provisions to ships from Japan and held large farming interests in Mexico.

The Sugar Beet and Farm Laborer's Union of Oxnard, California, was formed with Kusaburo Baba as president. When Secretary L.M. Larraras wrote the AFL for a charter, President Samuel Gompers replied, "Your union must guarantee that it will under no circumstances accept membership of any Chinese or Japanese."

1904   Hideyo Noguchi arrived in Philadelphia in 1900 from Japan. He then went to the Rockefeller Institute for Medical Research in New York City and was the first to demonstrate spirochetes of syphilis in the central nervous system of a dying patient.

March. Kentaro Kaneko was sent to the United States by the Japanese government to build popular support for Japan. He renewed his friendships with Roosevelt and Holmes, the President of the United States and an Associate Justice of the Supreme Court, respectively.

1905   Dr. Jokichi Takamine, the famous chemist, founded the Nip-
     pon Club in New York to improve understanding of U.S.-
     Japanese relations.

     February 23. The San Francisco Chronicle began a story
     under a front-page headline, "The Japanese Invasion, The
     Problem of the Hour." The anti-Japanese series continued
     on and off for over a year.

     March 1. The California state legislature urged the Cali-
     fornia delegation in Congress to introduce a resolution li-
     miting Japanese immigrants.

     May 7. Delegates from sixty-seven organizations met and
     launched the Asiatic Exclusion League in San Francisco.

     September 5. A peace treaty between Japan and Russia was
     signed at Portsmouth, New Hampshire, with the United States
     as mediator. This formally concluded the Russo-Japanese
     War begun in February in which Japan was the victor. This
     war also stimulated anti-Japanese feelings in the United
     States.

1906   San Francisco had an earthquake and in its aftermath more
     attacks and boycotts against the Japanese took place.

     Japan contributed $246,000, more than all other foreign
     nations combined, toward aiding the earthquake victims.

     Dr. F. Omori and Professor T. Nakamura of the Imperial
     University of Tokyo were sent by Japan to investigate the
     earthquake and were repeatedly stoned and attacked. They
     arrived at a time when strong anti-Japanese feelings pre-
     vailed.

     October 11. Mayor Eugene E. Schmitz and a political backer,
     Abraham Ruef, pressured the San Francisco school board
     to segregate ninety-three Japanese school children. Histor-
     ians have suggested this move was to divert attention from
     themselves as they were being probed by a grand jury over
     graft charges in the municipal government.

     Japanese Consul S. Uyeno filed a protest with the San Fran-
     cisco school board but was denied.

     October 21. Ambassador Luke Wright sent a worried tele-
     gram from Tokyo to Secretary of State Elihu Root reporting

Japan's negative reactions to the anti-Japanese occurrences in San Francisco.

October 25. Japan's Ambassador Shuzo Aoki conferred with Secretary Root to seek a solution to the problem involving San Francisco's segregated Oriental Public School.

October 26. President Theodore Roosevelt sent Secretary of Commerce and Labor Victor H. Metcalf to San Francisco to investigate how the rights of the Japanese could be protected.

October 31. Secretary Victor H. Metcalf arrived in San Francisco and found the school board charges against the Japanese students both contradictory and exaggerated.

December. Negotiation with Japan for a Gentleman's Agreement was begun. Its purpose was to limit the number of Japanese laborers entering the United States.

December 4. In his message to Congress, President Roosevelt berated San Francisco for its anti-Japanese acts and recommended that Congress pass an act allowing naturalization of the Japanese in America and amending civil and criminal statutes so that rights of aliens under treaty can be enforced.

1907 The Fresno Federated Trades & Labor Council, affiliated with the AFL, proposed an anti-Japanese resolution in a mailing.

February. Washington, D.C. invited the San Francisco school board to confer on the school segregation issue and on problems related to Japan. Mayor Schmitz, who was under indictment, accompanied Superintendent of Schools Roncovieri and President of the School Board Aaron Altman.

February 18. A pending immigration bill was amended to prevent Japanese laborers from entering the United States via Hawaii, Mexico, or Canada.

March 13. The San Francisco school board rescinded the school segregation order.

May. General Itei Kuroki and Vice Admiral Goro Ijuin from Japan were visiting the Jamestown Exposition when a

riot broke out against the Japanese in San Francisco, causing the United States government embarrassment.

June 27. The Board of Police Commissioners of San Francisco refused to license six Japanese to conduct employment
agency offices. The license requests were for four renew-
als and two new applications.

September. Over 1,800 Japanese laborers arrived in the
United States during this month.

October 14. In San Francisco another riot directed against
the Japanese residents took place.

October 25. President Roosevelt conferred with Ambassador
Aoki about the laborers from Japan still entering the United
States.

October 26. Secretary of State Root conferred with Ambassador Aoki to request stricter control over immigration
from Japan.

November. A total of 1,170 Japanese arrived in the United
States during this month.

December 11. Licenses were granted to the six Japanese
applicants for employment agencies in San Francisco by
the newly elected president of the Board of Police Commis-
sions.

December 16. The American fleet began its famous cruise
around the world principally to display its naval strength.

The mayor of San Francisco, Eugene Schmitz, and Abraham
Ruef were convicted of felony and jailed.

1908   For the year a total of 4,477 immigrants arrived in the
United States from Japan, but 5,035 Japanese left the United
States.

The Immigration Commission reported that in the decade
just ending 15,000 Japanese laborers were working on the
railroads.

There were 231 organizations now affiliated with the Asiatic
Exclusion League begun on May 7, 1905, of which 195 were
labor unions.

January. In Tokyo, Foreign Minister Kaoru Hayashi replied after a long waiting period to U.S. Ambassador O'Brien agreeing to the terms of immigration discussed in December, 1906, for a Gentlemen's Agreement.

January 28. Secretary of State Root's note that requested establishment of a registration system for emigrants was presented to Foreign Minister Hayashi.

February. For this month the total number of Japanese immigrants to the United States was 468.

March 9. Secretary Elihu Root instructed Ambassador O'Brien to thank Japan and thereby the negotiation of the Gentleman's Agreement begun in December, 1906, was concluded.

1909   When the California state legislature convened a number of racist measures were introduced, such as the prohibition against aliens owning land, the segregation of schools for Japanese children, and the establishment of ordinances to confine Orientals to ghettos.

Washington, D.C. became alarmed by the California legislature proposals because of their offensive tone to Japan and requested prevention of their passage via some twelve telegrams from President Roosevelt to Governor James N. Gillett.

Kintaro Sessue Hayakawa arrived in the United States and attended the University of Chicago.

The California legislature appropriated funds to investigate the Japanese in agriculture.

January 30. In Berkeley, California, Japanese residents were assaulted by white bigots.

March. Theodore Roosevelt completed his term as president. Japanese immigrant departures were still in excess of arrivals to the United States.

1910   The California state legislature introduced twenty-seven anti-Japanese proposals. Governor Hiram Johnson, urged by friends in the White House, persuaded the legislature not to pursue the proposals.

"Picture brides" began arriving for those Japanese men who requested wives from Japan. A proxy for the groom legalized the marriage in Japan and subsequently the bride emigrated to the United States.

By this time, the Japanese were producing about 70 percent of California's strawberries.

There were 79,786 Japanese in Hawaii, of whom some 20,000 were United States citizens or Nisei (those Japanese born on United States soil).

There were 72,157 Japanese on the mainland United States, of whom 4,502 were United States citizens or Nisei.

May. The California State Labor Commission submitted a report that was favorable to the Japanese. The Labor Commissioner was reprimanded publicly and his report was never published.

June 28. Arthur Kenzaburo Ozawa, a Nisei born in Hawaii, was admitted to the bar of Michigan after he graduated from the University of Michigan Law School.

July 29. Arthur Kenzaburo Ozawa was admitted to the bar of the Territory of Hawaii.

1911   President Taft intervened to prevent passage of anti-Japanese legislation in California since a treaty between Japan and the United States was under consideration.

San Francisco was planning a Pan-Pacific Exposition and desired Japan's participation, so the agitation against resident Japanese was temporarily eased.

1912   Masaharu Kondo arrived in San Diego, California, and became the president of M. & K. Fisheries Co., Mexican Industrial Development Co., and the Japanese Association. He was further involved with the San Diego Industrial Exposition and with the American War Relief organizations. Kondo's first visit to America had been in 1908 while on a world tour to study fishing and canning methods.

Sessue Hayakawa went to Los Angeles from Chicago and became part of the movie industry as an actor. Some of his many picture credits were The Cheat, The Bandit Prince,

Wrath of the Gods, and a Broadway play, Love City. He formed his own movie company called Imperial Picture Productions.

Yoneo Arai, a Nisei, graduated cum laude from Harvard University.

December 1. Minoru Yamasaki was born in Seattle, Washington.

1913   The California Alien Land Law was enacted. It was the first anti-Japanese land law. The original version denied ownership and leasing to "aliens ineligible to citizenship," but many white landowners wanted to lease their lands to Japanese tenants. In deference to the landowners, it was amended to read that leasing was to be limited to three years.

1914   Around this time, actor Masajiro Kaihatsu, known professionally as Yukio Aoyama, appeared in some sixty silent movies and serials. He was also an assistant director at the Vitagraph Studio. Later his son, Arthur Kaihatsu, appeared as a child actor in Hal Roach's Our Gang comedies.

The Federal Council of Churches and the Japan Society set up a Committee on Relations with Japan, which was directed by Reverend Sidney Gulick.

The Anti-Japanese campaign became subdued since Japan was an ally of the United States in World War I.

1915   September 28. The Hearst newspapers launched an anti-Japanese series with a piece entitled "Japan Plans to Invade and Conquer the U.S. . . . ".

October 15. Mike Masaru Masaoka was born in Fresno, California.

1916   The Hearst press continued its sensational anti-Japanese stories.

President Wilson requested withdrawal of the Hearst-produced movie Patria for its unfair anti-Japanese content calculated to stir hostilities.

1917   Arizona enacted a law similar to and based on the 1913 California Alien Land Law.

By this year, Japanese farmers on the West Coast had pioneered, developed, and introduced a variety of fruits and vegetables to an industrial production level.

June 21. Arthur Kenzaburo Ozawa, who was the first person of Japanese ancestry to be admitted to the practice of law within the jurisdiction of the United States and in the Territory of Hawaii, died.

1918   A small group of Nisei in San Francisco got together and called themselves the American Loyalty League in an attempt to seek solutions to discriminations against the Nisei.

Japanese Ambassador Viscount Kikujiro Ishii presented a samurai sword to Fairhaven, Massachusetts, in honor of Manjiro Nakahama, the first Japanese in the United States.

1919   The American Legion had its first convention at which a resolution was passed recommending exclusion of the Japanese.

V.S. McClatchy retired from his newspaper publishing business (Fresno Bee, Sacramento Bee) to devote all his time to anti-Japanese activities.

Production of the California Japanese farmers was $67 million, or one-tenth of California's output.

April 1. Two California Senators tried to introduce many anti-Japanese bills. Secretary of State Lansing requested their withdrawal since a peace conference was in session in Paris and Japan was an ally.

June 28. The Treaty of Versailles was signed. Anti-Japanese agitation began immediately in California.

September. V.S. McClatchy formed the California Joint Immigration Committee supported by the Native Sons of the Golden West, the Grange, the State Federation of Labor and the newly formed American Legion for an anti-Japanese campaign.

1920   The Alien Land Act of 1920 was passed wherein California tried to seal the loopholes in the 1913 Alien Land Law by forbidding the Japanese Issei to buy land in the name of their American-born children, the Nisei.

Ryuzaburo Ito received his master's degree from J.B. Stetson University in Florida. He continued his studies in theology and became the official interpreter of the Alameda County Court House, California, as well as an insurance man.

In a California newspaper The Fowler Ensign, an angry letter was published criticizing the successes of the Japanese farmers who consistently produced large yields from small acreages.

According to the Immigration Commission Reports, the number of Japanese railroad workers in the United States dropped to 4,300 from about 15,000 in 1908 as they moved onto other means of livelihood, such as farming, mining, and small businesses.

The Pride of Palomar by Peter B. Kyne and Seed of the Sun by Wallace Irwin were serialized in magazines. They portrayed despicable images of the Japanese.

July 12. Senator James D. Phelan conducted a hearing in San Francisco arranged by the Committee on Immigration and Naturalization, which proceeded to debase the Japanese.

September 10. The Federated Trades Council of Sacramento passed a resolution condemning anti-Japanese propaganda as detrimental to labor.

1921   Louisiana legislated a land law based on California's 1913 Alien Land Law.

V.S. McClatchy proposed and filed a brief for an exclusion act (against further Japanese immigration) with the United States Senate that was presented by Senator Hiram Johnson.

Around this time there were about 1,000 Japanese mining coal in central Utah.

Hidemitsu Toyota, an Issei who served in the United States military during World War I, was issued a certificate of naturalization in Massachusetts.

Japan enforced a "Ladies' Agreement" that was a voluntary halt to the practice, prevalent since 1910, of issuing passports to "picture brides."

Hachiro Onuki (Hutchlon Ohnick), the man who brought gas and electric power to the frontier town of Phoenix, Arizona, died.

The Seattle Progressive Citizens League was formed by Seattle's Nisei. Legalized discrimination through the use of the phrase "aliens ineligible to citizenghip," which was attached to many pieces of legislation, was the target of this league's efforts.

July 18. Several hundred white men rounded up fifty-eight Japanese laborers in Turlock, California, and boarded them on a train with a warning never to return. This began other similar forced removals of the Japanese.

1922   Congress passed the Cable Act, which provided that ". . . any woman citizen who marries an alien ineligible to citizenship shall cease to be a citizen of the U.S." This meant that a Nisei or a Caucasian woman who married an Issei lost her citizenship; but if this marriage terminated by divorce or death, the Caucasian woman could apply to regain her citizenship, whereas the Nisei woman could not because she was "of a race ineligible to citizenship."

New Mexico legislated a land law based on the 1913 California Alien Land Law.

James T. Harada was the first Nisei who ran for the territorial House seat in Hawaii, but lost.

November 13. The Supreme Court handed down its decision regarding Takao Ozawa's application for citizenship made in 1914. The Supreme Court upheld the 1790 Naturalization Law, which stated that the ". . . privilege of naturalization was confined to white persons." Inasmuch as Negroes were granted naturalization rights after the Civil War, Ozawa was therefore denied citizenship because he was neither white nor black.

1923   Idaho, Montana, and Oregon enacted land laws similar to the 1913 California Alien Land Law.

The American Loyalty League of Fresno, a California Nisei organization headed by Dr. Thomas T. Yatabe, was formed. It was credited as the original group of the Japanese American Citizens League (JACL).

The Congressional steering committee under V.S. McClatchy opened an office in Washington, D.C. to try for the passage of the Exclusion Act.

1924   March 15. The Immigration Exclusion Act was passed, which stated that all immigrants "ineligible for citizenship" were denied admission to the United States. This act limited all immigration to the United States, but denied all immigration from Japan.

September 7. Daniel Ken Inouye was born in Honolulu, Hawaii.

1925   Sojin Kamiyama, an actor, returned to Japan after having played the first Charlie Chan role and other roles that called for the Caucasian concept of the Oriental, which was one of being mysterious, sinister, and evil.

Hidemitsu Toyota, an Issei who served in the U.S. Coast Guard until May 1923, had his certificate of naturalization challenged. Although the act of 1918 gave "any alien" serv-in the U.S. armed forces, and the act of 1919 gave "any person of foreign birth," the right to naturalization, the Supreme Court denied Toyota's petition. They reasoned that since Sec. 2 of the Act of 1918 did not provide for repeal or for enlargement of the existing law (i.e. Sec. 2169) except as specified, then if the phrase "any alien" was to be taken literally, the qualifying words in Sec. 2169 ("being free white persons" and "of African nativity") would be without significance. Toyota was therefore denied naturalization although he served in the military, since he was neither white nor black.

Kansas passed an alien land law similar to California's 1913 Alien Land Law.

1926   Thomas T. Sakakihira, Republican from Hawaii, ran for the territorial House of Representatives, but lost.

George Shima, famous for his potatoes, died with an estimated estate of $15 million.

1927   James Yoshinori Sakamoto was the first Nisei to fight professionally at Madison Square Garden. He returned to Seattle, Washington, nearly blind from blows received in the ring.

1928   Clarence T. Arai, a Nisei attorney who was the president
of the Seattle Progressive Citizens League, went to Oregon
to help organize the all-Nisei Portland Progressive Citizens
League.

James Moriyama, T. Sakakihira, Harry Kurisaki and Leslie Nakashima, all Nisei Republicans, ran for the territorial House seats in Hawaii, but lost.

The Salons of America, Inc., of New York had among their
directors Yasuo Kuniyoshi, Kikuta Nakagawa, and Byron
Takashi Tsuzuki. The salon sponsored an exhibition that
included ten Japanese artists.

January 1. James Y. Sakamoto launched the Japanese American Courier, an all-English weekly, in Seattle. He called
for a reorganization of the Seattle Progressive Citizens
League.

August. Clarence Arai and George Ishihara were invited
to a conference by the American Loyalty League of Fresno
where they met Saburo Kido, Susumu Togasaki, Dr. Henry
Takahashi, and others. This united the Nisei of the Pacific
Northwest with the Pacific Southwest.

1929   April. Saburo Kido, an attorney, Thomas Yatabe, a den-
tist, and Clarence Arai, an attorney, proposed: (1) that a
national Nisei organization be formed; (2) that it be called
Japanese American Citizens League; and (3) that the founding convention be held in Seattle in the summer of 1930.

1930   The Japanese American Citizens League (JACL) held its
first convention with Clarence Arai as chairman. They
adopted resolutions to petition Congress to amend the Cable
Act and to grant citizenship to those Issei who served the
U.S. armed forces in World War I.

Suma Sugi, who represented the JACL, went to Washington,
D.C., and became the first Nisei lobbyist.

Noboru Miyake, a Nisei Republican, was elected county su-
pervisor in Hawaii.

Tasaku Oka, a Nisei Republican, was elected to the territorial House of Representatives in Hawaii.

Andy M. Yamashiro, a Nisei Democrat, was elected to the territorial House of Representatives in Hawaii.

1931   The Cable Act was amended allowing those Nisei women married to Issei to retain or regain their United States citizenship.

Japan entered the world market as a competitor whereby Californians felt threatened and renewed their anti-Japanese measures.

1932   The second national JACL convention was held in Los Angeles with Dr. George Y. Takeyama as chairman. Susumu Togasaki became its first treasurer and Saburo Kido its first executive secretary.

1933   Japan withdrew from the League of Nations.

1934   Tomekichi Okino was the first Nisei appointed to a judicial position as District Magistrate in Hawaii.

The JACL convention in San Francisco was headed by Chairman Dr. T. T. Hayashi. A constitutional provision for elective national officers was approved and Dr. T. Yatabe became its first elected president.

1935   Karl G. Yoneda was a farm labor organizer and author of History of Japanese Labor in the United States.

April 27. The Hearst newspapers renewed their vilification of the Japanese.

1936   Kyutaro Abiko, founder of Nichi Bei Times and the California Land Co. and one-time president of the Gospel Society of the Japanese Methodist Church, died.

There were nine Nisei among the ninety-three elected officials in Hawaii.

1937   The first major group of Japanese cannery workers was incorporated into a national union, the CIO, in Seattle.

AFL Local 770 of the Retail Food Clerks in California tried to organize the Nisei fruit-stand employees. The Nisei quickly organized a nonmilitant union of their own. The AFL, having failed and also having been stimulated by the anti-Japanese feelings in the United States due to Japan's invasion of China, began issuing handbills such as "Don't Buy Japanese."

1938 Hideichi Yamatoda, owner of the Tokyo Club in Los Angeles, was indicted on a murder charge along with several of his colleagues. The victim was a Tokyo Club client named Namba. They were convicted of manslaughter but the appellate court reversed the conviction; attorney Jerry Giesler defended Yamatoda and his friends.

The JACL held a convention in Los Angeles. Executive Secretary Walter Tsukamoto invited Mike Masaoka to speak. Masaoka constructively criticized the JACL and offered suggestions. President Jimmie Sakamoto asked Masaoka to leave as he was not an official delegate.

V.S. McClatchy, who devoted his energies to anti-Japanese activities, died.

1939 Mike Masaoka organized the Intermountain District Council as part of the JACL and was elected its chairman.

Minoru Yasui of Hood River, Oregon, graduated from the University of Oregon Law School but finding no employment to utilize his education, he began working for the Japanese Consulate in Chicago.

1940 The JACL held its convention in Portland, Oregon. Masaoka attended as a member of the National Board of JACL, which gave him a voice. He automatically qualified to be a member of the board by being a council chairman.

March 9. JACL leaders met with the Los Angeles City Council and pledged their support and loyalty and asked for a chance to demonstrate this.

March 21. JACL leaders met with officials of the Army and Navy Intelligence Services and offered their full cooperation.

1941 An independent Nisei union was given an AFL charter to organize all Japanese employees of retail produce and was granted the same contract as Local 770. The Nisei union voted to transfer.

May 9. The Japanese American Creed, written by Mike Masaoka in 1940, was published in the Congressional Record.

July 26. The United States abrogated the treaty of commerce and friendship with Japan and the assets of the Japanese nationals in the United States were frozen.

August. The JACL held a district council meeting and hired Mike Masaoka as its first staff employee. Masaoka resigned from his teaching position at the University of Utah.

The President's Commission on Equal Employment Opportunities held a hearing and invited the JACL. Masaoka testified to the discrimination against the hiring of qualified Nisei for defense jobs.

August. Ensign Takeo Yoshikawa, also known as Vice-Consul Morimura, was sent by Japan to report on United States ship movements in Pearl Harbor.

Thirty thousand Nisei with dual citizenships in Hawaii petitioned Secretary of State Cordell Hull to find the means to renounce their Japanese citizenship.

John Farnsworth, a former naval officer, and Harry Thomas Thompson, a former seaman, both native-born white Americans, were convicted of being espionage agents for Japan.

September. The War Department approved the creation of the Fourth Army Intelligence School with John Fujio Aiso as its head.

State Department representative Curtis B. Munson conferred privately with JACL President Saburo Kido and Mike Masaoka about the impending war with Japan and sought suggestions for the safety of the Japanese in the United States.

Kichisaburo Nomura and Saburo Kurusu were negotiating for Japan to have the United States lift the oil embargo, cease aid to China, and unfreeze Japanese assets and in return to have Japan withdraw from Indochina after China had come to terms. Secretary of State Cordell Hull refused.

December 7. Japan bombed Pearl Harbor.

JACL President Kido sent a telegram to President Franklin D. Roosevelt pledging loyalty and support of the Nisei.

Governor Ralph Carr of Colorado was the only one among

the western governors who gave support to the Japanese in
the United States.

While on a speaking tour, Mike Masaoka was jailed in North
Platte, Nebraska. Senator Elbert Thomas of Utah arranged
for Masaoka's release and for the trip to San Francisco.
En route in Cheyenne, Wyoming, Masaoka was again jailed.
Senator Thomas again intervened and this time provided
him with an FBI escort.

December 8. Togo Tanaka, editor of the Rafu Shimpo, was
arrested by FBI agents. He was in three different jails in
eleven days but was never charged.

December 15. Secretary of the Navy Frank Knox said at a
press conference, "I think the most effective fifth column
work of the entire war was done in Hawaii, with the possible
exception of Norway," although his official report contained
no mention of fifth column activity.

December 19. Lt. Gen. J.L. DeWitt, commander of the
Western Defense Commands, recommended the removal of
enemy aliens over fourteen years old from the West Coast,
which he approximated at 40,000. It was therefore clear
that DeWitt thought only in terms of the Japanese, for "all
alien subjects of enemy nations" on the West Coast should
have included 58,000 Italians and 23,000 Germans as well
as the 40,000 Japanese.

Maj. Gen. Allen W. Gullion, Provost Marshal General in
Washington, D.C., was requested by the Los Angeles Chamber of Commerce to round up all Japanese in the Los Angeles area.

December. Many Issei were taken from their homes and
places of business with no warnings by the FBI agents.
Many had their homes searched by FBI agents. In four days,
Japanese detainees totalled 1,370.

Many efforts were made to proclaim the loyalty of the
United States Japanese but were ineffective.

The Treasury Department blocked the financial activities
of Japanese aliens. Bank accounts bearing Japanese-sound-
ing names were frozen causing many hardships. Through
the JACL and Senator Thomas, the Treasury Department
eased its orders and allowed withdrawals of up to $100 per
month.

The army honorably discharged without specification a number of Nisei who had been inducted before December 7.
They were given a 4-F classification (ineligible because of
physical defect).

1942   Frederick Vincent Williams and David Warren Ryder, a
Pacific Coast journalist, were charged and convicted of being
unregistered agents of Japan.

Damon Runyon, Walter Lippman, Henry McLemore and
Westbrook Pegler were among the majority of news commen-
tators who warned of disloyalty of the Japanese in the United
States. Ernie Pyle and Chester Rowell were among the minority who urged fair play toward the United States Japanese.

January. Minoru Yasui, a commissioned lieutenant with
college ROTC, received orders for active duty at Ft. Van-
couver, Washington, and was put in charge of a platoon.
Within twenty-four hours, Yasui was released by the Army
as unacceptable.

January. California Governor Culbert Olson held a meeting
with twenty-four Nisei leaders and proposed moving the Japanese inland and allowing them to continue to produce food
". . . for their own good." Saburo Kido suggested if Olson
were so concerned with the Japanese welfare, he should provide for police protection as the Japanese continued to live
in their homes. The meeting ended with Olson complaining
about the lack of gratitude and cooperation from the Nisei.

January 5. John B. Hughes, radio commentator, criticized
the Justice Department and suggested the evacuation of all
Japanese.

January 21. Congressman Leland Ford was the first congressman to advocate, from the House floor, mass evacuation of the United States Japanese.

January 29. U.S. Attorney Gen. Francis Biddle ordered the
establishment of Pacific Coast strategic areas in order to
remove all enemy aliens.

January 30. Col. Karl Bendetsen, representative of the War
Department, appeared before the West Coast Congressional
delegation and endorsed the Japanese evacuation.

February. Attorney General of California Earl Warren recommended tightening the Alien Land Law as a step in dis-
placing the Japanese residents. Fifty-nine escheat proceedings out of seventy-nine were begun at Warren's urging.

February 10. Senator Mon C. Wallgren's committee wrote
a resolution recommending the mass evacuation of the
United States Japanese.

Attorney Gen. Biddle received opinions of attorneys Cohen,
Cox, and Rauh upholding the legality of evacuation under the
president's war powers.

February 11. Secretary of War Henry L. Stimson ordered
his assistant, John J. McCloy, who in turn ordered Col. Karl
Bendetsen, to set the evacuation of all West Coast Japanese
into motion. This was done despite opinions of "no further
dangers of a Pacific Coast invasion" from top Army and Navy
commanders. In his own words, Bendetsen said that it was
he who " . . . conceived method, formulated details and directed evacuation of 120,000 persons of Japanese ancestry
. . ."

February 13. A West Coast delegation rewrote the Wallgren resolution by adding that the evacuees were to be of
"Japanese lineage." A Southern trio in Congress, Senator
Tom Stewart of Tennessee and Representatives John Rankin
of Mississippi and Martin Dies of Texas, gave support to
the Pacific Coast delegation.

The West Coast congressional delegation sent a letter to
President Roosevelt recommending immediate evacuation of
the Japanese from the entire West Coast.

February 14. Lt. Gen. J. DeWitt sent a memo to Secretary
Stimson recommending evacuation of Japanese and other subversive persons from the West Coast area.

The Navy posted notice that all Japanese on Terminal Island,
California, were to evacuate by March 14.

February 17. Attorney Gen. Biddle sent a memo to President Roosevelt that was a summation, discussion, and recommendation of the West Coast situation involving the Japanese residents. Biddle recommended clarification of facts
to the public to counteract the writings of some dangerous

and irresponsible columnists and he opposed mass evacuation.

February 19. President Roosevelt signed Executive Order No. 9066. This authorized the Secretary of War or his designated military commander to establish military areas and to exclude people from military areas. This order uprooted 110,000 people of Japanese ancestry.

February 20. Secretary Stimson designated General DeWitt to carry out the evacuation of the Japanese on the West Coast under the terms of Executive Order No. 9066.

February 21. Representative John H. Tolan and his committee opened hearings in San Francisco to investigate the problems of evacuation. In the San Francisco session, nine persons of Japanese ancestry were heard out of forty-three witnesses. In the Portland-Seattle sessions, four Japanese out of fifty witnesses were heard. Mike Masaoka made a statement on behalf of the JACL, opposing evacuation except as a military necessity. Masaoka, Henry Tani, and Dave Tatsuno were questioned about their personal lives, which had little to do with solving the "problems of evacuation."

February 23. A Japanese submarine shelled oil installations at Goleta, California.

February 25. New posters were put up on Terminal Island, California ordering the Japanese off the island by midnight of February 27 thus cancelling the month's notice provided in the February 14 order.

March 2. General DeWitt issued Proclamation No. 1 designating the western half of the three Pacific Coast states and the southern third of Arizona as military area number 1 and the eastern half of the three Pacific Coast states and the northern parts of Arizona as military area number 2, from which all persons of Japanese descent were to be removed.

March 11. General DeWitt established the Wartime Civil Control Administration (WCCA) with Colonel Bendetsen as director to carry out the Japanese evacuation.

March 12. The Tolan Committee ended hearings in San Francisco, having held hearings in Portland, Seattle, and Los Angeles. During one of the sessions, Attorney General

of California Earl Warren pointed out on a map the proxim-
ity of Japanese residences to strategic installations. Warren failed to mention that these Japanese were established
well before any installations were placed, for since the end
of the 1800s, the Japanese were engaged in converting these
then unwanted and unused lands into fertile, viable lands
for farming.

March 18. President Roosevelt signed Executive Order No.
9102 which created the War Relocation Authority (WRA)
naming Milton S. Eisenhower as director; its purpose was
to look after the Japanese evacuees from the West Coast.

March 21. President Roosevelt signed Public Law No. 503
making any violation of an order of the military commander,
as specified under Executive Order No. 9066, a misdemeanor.

March 22. The first group of Japanese from Los Angeles
was evacuated to Manzanar Assembly Center, California,
by the Army.

March 23. General DeWitt issued Civilian Exclusion Order
No. 1 which ordered the removal of the Japanese from Bainbridge Island, Washington, by March 30.

March 24. Posters ordering the Japanese to leave in six
days were put up on Bainbridge Island, Washington.

General DeWitt issued a curfew order for all Japanese to be
confined to their homes daily between 8:00 P.M. and 6:00
A.M.

March 27. General DeWitt issued Proclamation No. 4 forbidding further voluntary migration of the Japanese from the
established military areas due to the hostility of the general
public of the inland areas.

March 30. The army removed fifty-four Japanese families
from Bainbridge Island, Washington, to Manzanar Assembly
Center, California.

The Nisei men were reclassified and exempted from draft
in a 4-F classification.

Gordon Hirabayashi, a Nisei, was arrested by federal authorities and was convicted of having violated both army orders (curfew and evacuation) in Washington.

Minoru Yasui, a Nisei, deliberately got himself arrested in Portland, Oregon, to test the curfew violation.

April 7. The Intermountain Conference, known as the "Governors' Conference," included representatives from ten western states, Milton Eisenhower of the WRA and Colonel Bendetsen of the WCCA. In discussing resettlement plans, the majority protested the relocation of Japanese people into their own particular states. The protestations were short-lived as the need for agricultural labor was keen. This forced the WRA to drop plans for many small temporary camps and to settle on fewer large semipermanent camps.

May 8. The first group of evacuees assigned to the Colorado River Relocation Center (Poston) near Parker, Arizona, arrived.

May 21. Fifteen Japanese from the Portland Army Assembly Center went to Malheur County, Oregon, to do seasonal farming. They were under civilian restriction order of the Western Defense Command.

May 27. The first group of evacuees assigned to Tule Lake Relocation Center, California, arrived.

May 29. The National Student Relocation Council to help the Nisei continue their education was formed through the aid of Clarence Pickett. President John W. Nason of Swarthmore College was the chairman. The headquarters was in Philadelphia.

$70,000 was seized from the Japanese Association of New York by the federal government.

June 1. The Fourth Army Intelligence School to teach the Japanese language was moved from San Francisco to Camp Savage, Minnesota, and was reorganized as Military Intelligence Service Language School.

The Manzanar Army Assembly Center was renamed Manzanar Relocation Center when it was transferred from WCCA to WRA.

June 2. General DeWitt issued Public Proclamation No. 6, which prevented further voluntary migration from eastern California and declared these Japanese would be placed in WRA centers.

June 4. Those of Japanese ancestry serving in the Hawaiian National Guard, now called the 100th Infantry Battalion, were sent to Camp McCoy, Wisconsin.

June 5. All Japanese were removed from Military Area No. 1, which was the western half of Washington, Oregon, and California and southern Arizona.

June 17. The War Department declared the Nisei to be unacceptable for service in the armed forces "except as may be authorized in special cases."

Milton Eisenhower resigned as Director of WRA to become Deputy Director of the Office of War Information, and President Roosevelt appointed Dillon S. Myer to replace Eisenhower.

June 20. WRA adopted its first leave policy enabling certain evacuees to leave relocation camps.

A Japanese submarine fired on shore batteries near Astoria, Oregon.

July. James Purcell, attorney, filed a writ of habeas corpus with the federal court in San Francisco in behalf of Mitsuye Endo, a Nisei civil service employee, to test the legality of incarcerating a loyal citizen against her will when accused of nothing.

August 7. All Japanese were removed from Military Area No. 2, which was the eastern half of the three Pacific Coast states and the northern part of Arizona.

August 10. Minidoka Relocation Center, Idaho, received its first group of evacuees from Puyallup Army Assembly Center.

August 12. Heart Mountain Relocation Center, Wyoming, received its first group of evacuees from Pomona Army Assembly Center.

August 27. Granada Relocation Center, Colorado, opened with evacuees from Merced Army Assembly Center.

September. When the WRA circulated an honest and a complete story of the evacuation, job offers to the Japanese began to trickle in. Issei railroad workers of eastern Oregon were offered their former jobs.

The American Legion convention in Kansas City protested the WRA encouragement for educational and agricultural jobs out of the camps and urged that all evacuees be kept confined.

September 1. The Army changed the Nisei 4-F classification (ineligible because of physical defect) to 4-C (ineligible because of nationality or ancestry).

September 9. Japan's submarine-based plane bombed Mount Emily in Oregon in an attempt to start a fire.

September 11. The Central Utah Relocation Center (Topaz, Utah) received its first group of evacuees from Tanforan Army Assembly Center.

September 18. Rohwer Relocation Center, Arkansas, received its first group of evacuees from Stockton Army Assembly Center, California.

September 26. WRA laid a basis for a resettlement program and revised and expanded its basic leave regulation.

October 6. Jerome Relocation Center, Arkansas, received its first group of evacuees from Fresno Army Assembly Center.

October. About 10,000 Japanese evacuees from various centers were out of the camps on "seasonal leave" to help harvest sugar beets and other produce. Local officials criticized WRA and evacuees for not providing more manpower.

November. Minoru Yasui was tried for violating a curfew order in Portland, Oregon. The court said although there was a precedent whereby the military could not bind civilians without declaration of martial law, it did not apply to Yasui since unbeknownst to him, he had been stripped of his United States citizenship, having been employed by the Japanese Consulate.

November. JACL held a conference in Salt Lake City with two representatives from each camp. Mike Masaoka, backed by Saburo Kido, proposed conscription for all Nisei men as a "right" of Nisei to serve in the military as any other American.

Saburo Kido (Poston Center), Thomas Yatabe (Jerome Center), Professor Obata and Rev. Taro Goto (Topaz Center) and Fred Tayama were severely beaten in response to the proposed conscription by those who already felt betrayed by the United States government for their incarceration.

November 3. Transfer of Army WCCA to WRA was completed.

November 14. "The Poston Incident" was a strike and a demonstration protesting the arrest of two evacuees beating a third at Poston Relocation Center, Arizona.

November 15. WRA announced its plans to eliminate its regional offices.

December 6. The Military Police took temporary control of Manzanar Relocation Center to stop demonstrations over the question of conscription. In this confusion a twenty-two-year old and a seventeen-year old were killed and many were injured, which left a pall over the camp.

December 10. From Manzanar Center the small group of agitators was sent to Moab, Utah, and the pro-American group was sent to Death Valley, California, for their safety.

December 31. The Hawaiian Nisei of the 100th Infantry Battalion were ordered from Camp McCoy to Camp Shelby, Mississippi.

There were 1,875 Japanese from Hawaii interned in camps on the mainland, of whom 981 had been rounded up by the FBI immediately following the bombing of Pearl Harbor.

More than 2,100 Japanese, mostly from Peru and the rest from other parts of South America, were deported to the United States and placed in various relocation centers. Gen. George C. Marshall requested these Japanese in the event an exchange might take place involving American citizens in countries held by Japan.

1943   Ralph Townsend, a leader in the America First movement, was sentenced to jail as an unregistered agent of Japan.

January. The majority of the Nisei men who remained in uniform were ordered to Camp Shelby, Mississippi.

January 1. The WRA established field offices to facilitate evacuees relocating out of camps.

January 20. The Senate Committee on Military Affairs appointed a subcommittee to investigate the WRA program and to consider transferring WRA to the War Department.

January 28. Secretary of War Stimson announced a new policy of ". . . inherent rights of every faithful citizen regardless of ancestry to bear arms in the national defense . . .," which was a plan to form an all-Japanese-American combat team with volunteers from the United States and Hawaii to be designated the 442nd Regimental Combat Team.

February 1. President Roosevelt wrote to Secretary Stimson praising the decision to form an all-Nisei combat team. (This letter was drafted by the WRA with the most quoted sentence authored by the head of the Office of War Information, Elmer Davis, which was, "The principle on which this country was founded and by which it has always been governed is that Americanism is a matter of the mind and heart; Americanism is not, and never was, a matter of race or ancestry.")

February 8. Loyalty registration for Army enlistment began at most relocation centers. The WRA in haste used this same questionnaire (intended only for Nisei men) to process those living in camps for leave clearance in seeking life out of the centers. However questions 27 and 28 regarding loyalty brought about much confusion. Question 27 asked if the evacuee were willing to serve the United States armed forces in combat and many women answered "No"; others gave a qualified "Yes," i.e. if they could in fact be treated as a citizen and be able to live anywhere in the United States. Question 28 asked if the evacuee would forswear allegiance to the Japanese emperor or to Japan and swear unqualified allegiance to the United States and many Issei replied "No," for at this point the Issei were denied naturalization and to have answered "Yes" would thus make them stateless.

March 11. WRA Director Dillon S. Myer wrote to Secretary Stimson urging relaxation of the West Coast exclusion orders against the Japanese.

March 20. WRA project directors were authorized to issue leave permits to those Japanese cleared by the Washington, D.C., office, who wished to relocate.

April 8. Senator A.B. Chandler of Kentucky, a member of the subcommittee investigating the WRA, wrote to WRA Director Myer recommending the segregation of the "disloyal" evacuees.

April. In April 2,686 Hawaiian Nisei volunteers arrived at Camp Shelby, Mississippi.

April 11. James Hatsuaki Wakasa was shot and killed by a Military Police sentry in Topaz Relocation Center when he innocently walked too close to the barbed wire fence.

April 13. General DeWitt testified before the House Naval Affairs Subcommittee in San Francisco stating: " . . . A Jap's a Jap. They are a dangerous element, whether loyal or not. There is no way to determine their loyalty . . . It makes no difference whether he is an American; theoretically he is still a Japanese . . . You can't change him by giving him a piece of paper."

April 19. General DeWitt issued Public Proclamation No.17 which authorized Nisei soldiers to return to the West Coast while on furlough or leave.

May 6. Eleanor Roosevelt visited the Gila River Relocation Center for the day.

May 10. Secretary of War Stimson rejected WRA Director Myer's recommendation of March 11 and strongly urged segregation.

May 25. Subsequent to processing the leave clearance questionnaire, an announcement was made to transfer all "disloyal" evacuees from the other centers (about 9,000) to the Tule Lake Center and the "loyals" of Tule Lake (about 9,000) to be dispersed into other centers. The "disloyals" were those who wished to be repatriated and expatriated to Japan for various reasons.

June 3. Chairman Martin Dies of the Committee on Un-American Activities appointed a three-man subcommittee to investigate the WRA.

June 8. The Dies Subcommittee hearings opened.

June 14. The Office of War Information revealed that Nazi agents were signaling Japanese planes at Pearl Harbor on December 6, 1941, the eve of Japan's attack.

June 25. WRA Director Dillon Myer wrote to Assistant Secretary of War McCloy about the segregation program and the selection of Tule Lake Relocation Center for the segregation center for those evacuees who wished to be repatriated or expatriated to Japan.

July. Judge Michael J. Roche denied petition on the Mitsuye Endo case.

July 6. WRA Director Myer appeared before the "Costello Committee" (same as the Dies Committee but Rep. J. Costello was chairman of the West Coast hearings, hence the name). Myer defended the administration of the WRA.

July 9. Heizer Wright, a member of the editorial staff of the New York Daily News was indicted as an unregistered agent for Japan.

August. The Supreme Court heard the appeals of Minoru Yasui and Gordon Hirabayashi. On Yasui, the Court ruled he had not lost his citizenship and the Army did have authority in the absence of martial law. On Hirabayashi, the Court ruled only on the curfew order and found him guilty; the Court refused to rule on the constitutionality of the evacuation order.

September 2. The all-Nisei 100th Battalion landed at Oran, North Africa, and was involved in heavy combat.

October 11. The final group of "disloyal" evacuees arrived at the Tule Lake Center, California.

October 19. Before a California state senate committee, Dr. John Carruthers, a Presbyterian minister, said, "It is our Christian duty to keep the Japanese out of this western world of Christian civilization . . ."

November 4. A riot, touched off by a truck accident where-in several were injured and one died, provided grist for a group of dissidents to push for various demands at the Tule Lake Relocation Center. This brought in troops as WRA temporarily transferred control to the Army.

November 24. WRA Director Myer testified about the Tule Lake disturbance before the Senate Committee on Military Affairs.

December. Both Los Angeles newspapers, the Examiner and the Times, in their campaign to keep the evacuees from returning to California, repeatedly carried exaggerated headlines of false and degrading stories about the United States Japanese.

December. Senator Jack Tenney of Los Angeles County be-gan to conduct his own hearings, as the "Little Dies Com-mittee." Shortly Rep. Chester Gannon of Sacramento formed his own Gannon Committee. Both of these commit-tees badgered witnesses who asked for fair play for the evacuees.

December. The State Board of Agriculture passed a resolu-tion in favor of returning the evacuees to California and urging fair treatment. Three members of the board were appointees of former Governor Olson. Governor Earl War-ren appointed new members to the board to effect a rever-sal of this resolution.

December 2. In the Korematsu v. U.S. case, the Ninth Circuit Court upheld the evacuation order as constitutional.

1944

The attorney general of California filed an escheat case against Kajiro Oyama, charging violation of the anti-alien land law.

January 7. Arthur Clifford Reed, a native-born white Ameri-can and a former corporal in the Army, was indicted as an unregistered agent of Japan.

January 14. Military control was ended at Tule Lake Center.

January 20. Secretary of War Stimson announced that Ja-panese Americans would be drafted through the regular Se-lective Service due to the record achieved by other Nisei in the Army.

February 16. President Roosevelt signed Executive Order No. 9423 which transferred the WRA to the Department of Interior.

March 18. Congressman Herman P. Eberharter said that public fears and antagonism were hampering WRA operations; that the Dies investigations fostered a type of racial thinking that was producing an ugly manifestation, and that the investigation should be checked before it became a shameful blot on our national record.

May. The 100th Battalion became the first battalion of the 442nd Combat Team.

May 24. Shoichi James Okamoto was shot and killed by an army sentry at the Tule Lake Center following an argument about passes.

June 2. The all-Nisei 442nd Combat Team landed in Italy.

June 30. Jerome Relocation Center, Arkansas, was closed.

July 1. President Roosevelt signed Public Law No. 405, which permitted American citizens to renounce their citizenship in time of war.

July 2. Takeo Noma was murdered at Tule Lake Center by unknown assasins.

October 11, 12. The Supreme Court heard oral arguments by Wayne Collins in the Fred Korematsu case.

October 12. The Supreme Court heard oral arguments by James Purcell in the Mitsuye Endo case.

October 18. Following the capture of Bruyeres, France, the 442nd Combat Team rescued the "Lost Battalion" of Texas, after a fierce battle in which the 442nd suffered heavy casualties.

December 17. The War Department announced the revocation of the West Coast mass exclusion order against persons of Japanese descent.

December 18. The WRA announced that all relocation centers would be closed by the end of 1945.

The Korematsu and Endo decisions were returned: Korematsu was found guilty of violating Civilian Exclusion Order
No. 34 and Endo was ordered released from camp, for having been found a loyal citizen the WRA could not detain her
against her will. In short, the Supreme Court ruled both
that evacuation was constitutional and that loyal Nisei were
free to move anywhere across the United States including
the West Coast from which the army lifted the ban just the
day before.

1945   The Teamsters Union boycotted Japanese produce until the
            end of 1945.

            The California Board of Equalization refused to issue com-
            mercial licenses to Japanese until the WRA threatened to
            file suit.

            Final count of Hawaii's war casualties showed 80 percent
            of those killed and 88 percent of those wounded were of Ja-
            panese ancestry. These figures included those on the home
            front as well as those in the Pacific and European theaters
            of operations.

            January 8. In Placer County, California, a Japanese fruit
            packing shed was dynamited. This was the first of thirty-
            six authenticated instances of violence against the returning
            Japanese people.

            April 5. A posthumous Medal of Honor was awarded to Pfc.
            Sadao S. Munemori for heroism in combat in Italy.

            May 14. Secretary of the Interior Harold L. Ickes publicly
            denounced the West Coast terrorism against the returning
            Japanese and urged stronger local law enforcement.

            August 6. The United States released its first atomic bomb
            on Hiroshima, Japan.

            August 9. The United States atom-bombed Nagasaki, Japan.

            August 15. Japan accepted Allied surrender terms (VJ Day).

            August 27. The American Occupational Force entered Japan.

            September 2. Japan formally surrendered aboard the U.S.S.
            Missouri in Tokyo Bay.

            September 4. The Western Defense Command issued Public Proclamation No. 24 revoking exclusion orders and military restrictions against persons of Japanese ancestry.

December. The Distinguished Service Cross was posthumously awarded to Sgt. Kazuo Masuda for heroic deeds in Italy. It was personally presented by Gen. Stilwell to Mary Masuda, the sergeant's sister.

1946   California Attorney Gen. Robert W. Kenny charged one sheriff with malfeasance for acts directed against the returning Japanese.

The first postwar JACL convention in Denver, Colorado, set as its goals naturalization for the Issei, revision of the 1924 Immigration Law, and indemnity for losses suffered from evacuation.

Saburo Kido, attorney and one of the early leaders of the JACL, received the Selective Service Medal for patriotism.

January 7. Attorney Gen. Tom C. Clark announced lifting restrictions against alien Japanese. This meant the Issei would no longer need to carry I. D. cards or report changes of address or employment.

February 23. The last group of the "disloyals" were repatriated from Tule Lake Center. They sailed to Japan from Long Beach, California, and numbered 432.

March 20. Tule Lake Segregation Center was closed.

May 8. WRA Director Dillon S. Myer received the "Medal for Merit" for his work with the WRA during the war.

June 30. The WRA program was officially ended.

July 15. President Truman presented the returning Nisei men of the 442nd Regimental Combat Team the Presidential Distinguished Unit Citation after they paraded on Constitution Avenue. The 442nd Infantry Regiment was the most decorated group of World War II.

August 8. The New York American Committee for Japan Relief was formed.

November 5. The JACL Anti-Discrimination Committee sought to attack California's Proposition 15, "Validation of Legislative Amendments to Alien Land Law," which attempted to reconfirm the Alien Land Law of 1913. The measure was defeated.

1947   May 3. Japan adopted a new constitution in which it re-
        nounced the right to wage war.

        Fall. In Takahashi v. Fish and Game Commission, the Su-
        preme Court ruled section 990 of the Fish and Game Code
        of California unconstitutional. Takahashi was granted a com-
        mercial fishing license as a right to make a living.

1948   In The People v. Oyama, the U.S. Supreme Court ruled
        the California escheat action unconstitutional.

        July 2. President Truman signed the Japanese American
        Evacuation Claims Act, enabling evacuees to file claims
        against the federal government for financial losses suffered
        in the evacuation.

        December 23. Gen. Hideki Tojo was hanged for war crimes
        in Japan.

1949   The Japanese American Welfare Society, also known as the
        Kyosai Kai, was founded. It primarily served the Japanese
        restaurant workers of New York.

        Dr. Hideki Yukawa received the Nobel Physics Prize on his
        meson theory. He taught at Princeton Institute for Advanced
        Study and at Columbia University and returned to Japan in
        1953.

        October 7. Iva Toguri D'Aquino, also known as "Tokyo
        Rose," was sentenced in San Francisco to ten years in pri-
        son for treason.

1950   At JACL's request, Congressman Walter H. Judd introduced
        a resolution to authorize naturalization of any qualified alien
        regardless of race or nationality.

        The Internal Security Act, also known as the McCarran Act,
        became law, despite objections by Senator McCarran and
        the JACL and despite President Truman's veto. This act
        was a compilation of amendments attached to the proposed
        resolution. This act which included Title II, otherwise
        known as the "concentration camp measure," was authored
        by Representative Sam Hobbs of Alabama.

        The JACL began awarding "Nisei of the Biennium" as well
        as citing other deserving Nisei. For their first Nisei of

the Biennium, JACL chose Mike Masaru Masaoka for his
dedication and sacrifices to the Japanese cause in myriad
ways beginning in 1938. Others cited were Saburo Kido,
Setsuko Nishi, Hito Okada, and Larry Tajiri.

1951

MGM produced a movie Go For Broke, which publicized the
deeds of the heroic Nisei of the 442nd Combat Regiment.

The New York American Committee for Japan Relief re-
grouped and adopted a new name, The Japanese American
Committee of New York, Inc., which was engaged in aiding
the Issei of the New York City area.

September. The San Francisco Peace Treaty conference
was held and several topics were discussed: Japan's right
to self defense, United States forces remaining in Japan until she could defend herself, Japan's recognition of the independence of Korea and Japan's renouncing of all rights to
Formosa, Kuriles, and South Sakhalin.

1952

The Kyosai Kai and the Japanese American Welfare Society
merged and became the Japanese Association of New York,
Inc.

Tommy Kono won the Olympic gold medal for weight-lifting
in the lightweight division at Helsinki, Finland.

Ford Hiroshi Konno won the 1500-meter free-style swim-
ming match in the Olympics at Helsinki, Finland.

Robert Murakami was appointed to the Circuit Court in Hawaii.

John F. Aiso served as a commissioner in the Superior
Court in California.

The JACL chose Minoru Yasui as the Nisei of the Biennium
for sacrifices made in challenging the legality of the army
curfew order and for serving the JACL as the Denver regional director. Also honored were Tomi Kanazawa, Ford
Hiroshi Konno, K. Patrick Okura, Bill Hosokawa, and Carl
Sato.

April. The San Francisco Peace Treaty between the United
States and Japan became effective.

July 27. The Walter-McCarran Immigration and Naturalization Act provided for repeal of the Oriental Exclusion Act of 1924. It extended token immigration quotas to Japan and to other Asian nations.

1953   The federal government returned $52,125 to the Japanese American Association of New York, Inc. in reparation for the $70,000 seized from the original Japanese Association of New York.

Takeshi Yoshihara became the first Nisei to graduate from the U.S. Naval Academy.

Sgt. Hiroshi Hershey Miyamura, after his release from a North Korean P.O.W. camp, was cited as one of the "Ten Outstanding Men in the United States in 1953" by the U.S. Junior Chamber of Commerce.

September 25. John F. Aiso was the first mainland Nisei named to a judicial post, the Municipal Court in Los Angeles, by Governor Earl Warren.

1954   Sgt. Hiroshi Hershey Miyamura was presented the Medal of Honor by President Eisenhower for heroic deeds performed on April 24, 1951, in Korea.

South American deportees of Japanese descent were allowed to apply for a permanent residence status in the United States. Peru refused them reentry. The ACLU helped.

Masaji Marumoto was elected president of the Hawaiian Bar Association.

Daniel K. Inouye was majority leader (until 1958) in the territorial house of representatives in Hawaii.

Spark Matsunaga served in the territorial legislature of Hawaii (until 1959).

The JACL chose Hiroshi Hershey Miyamura as the Nisei of the Biennium. Others cited were John F. Aiso, Dr. Minol Ota, Rev. Jitsuo Morikawa, and Thomas Yego, with special awards to Dr. Harvey Itano and George Iwashita.

1955   Robert Sakata was named "One of America's Four Outstanding Young Farmers in 1955" by the U.S. Junior Chamber of

Commerce. He was also chairman of the Brighton Agricultural Conference, advisor to Future Farmers of America, and an officer of the Brighton, Colorado, Junior Chamber of Commerce.

Jimmie Sakamoto, a boxer and publisher, died.

March. Shigeo Wakamatsu was named "Man of the Month" by the Lever Bros. Co., where he was a chemist.

1956 Masaji Marumoto became the first Nisei justice of the State Supreme Court in Hawaii.

Tommy Kono won an Olympic gold medal for weight-lifting in the light heavyweight division at Melbourne, Australia.

Patsy Takemoto Mink was elected to the territorial house of representatives in Hawaii.

The JACL chose George Inagaki as the Nisei of the Biennium for community consciousness in being involved in the Los Angeles Welfare Council, Southern California Japanese Children's Home, Adoption Bureau, and for service as national JACL president from 1952 to 1956. Also cited were Jack Murata, Minoru Yamasaki, Robert Sakata, and Shigeo Wakamatsu.

January 28. I. Toguri D'Aquino ("Tokyo Rose") was paroled.

December 19. Japan was elected the eightieth member of the United Nations.

1957 Patsy Takemoto Mink was elected vice-president of the Young Democrats of America (until 1959).

James Kanno was the first Nisei elected as mayor of Fountain City, Orange County, California.

Sessue Hayakawa starred in Bridge on the River Kwai, which won three Academy Awards.

1958 Daniel K. Inouye served in the territorial senate in Hawaii (until 1959).

The JACL chose Bill Hosokawa as the Nisei of the Biennium. He was assistant managing editor of the Denver Post, its first foreign correspondent who covered the Korean War, and president of the American Association of Sunday and Feature Editors. Also awarded were Harry Ayao Osaki, Tommy Kono, Tom Shimasaki, and Dr. Iwao Milton Moriyama.

Dr. Hatsuji James Hara received the Medal of Honor for Americanism from the DAR.

1959   Hawaii became the fiftieth state of the union.

Daniel K. Inouye was elected Hawaii's first representative with it became the first Nisei in Congress.

K. Patrick Okura was appointed chief probation officer of Douglas County, Omaha Juvenile Court.

Tom Kitayama was elected mayor of Union City, California.

Wilfred C. Tsukiyama became Hawaii's first chief justice.

1960   Daniel K. Inouye was elected Hawaii's first representative and with it became the first Nisei in Congress.

Leslie Benji Nerio joined the staff of the Honolulu Academy of Arts and became curator of Oriental art.

The JACL chose Daniel K. Inouye as the Nisei of the Biennium for his contributions through politics. Also honored were Pat Suzuki, Stephen Tamura, David Tatsuno, and Rev. Donald Toriumi.

January 19. Premier Nobusuke Kishi signed a new treaty with President Eisenhower. This ten-year Treaty of Mutual Cooperation and Security replaced the 1952 treaty. It provided for the United States use of military bases in Japan without time limitation, agreed upon economic cooperation as well as peaceful settlement of disputes.

June 2. Japan's Kabuki Theatre visited New York and California to participate in the one hundredth anniversary celebration of the United States-Japan Treaty of Amity and Commerce.

1961   Yosuke W. (Nick) Nakano died. He came to America in 1887, attended various schools and joined Philadelphia's

Wark & Co. as chief engineer. Nakano helped develop a process for pouring concrete into forms for large buildings and was involved in erecting more than two hundred major buildings on the East Coast.

1962   Daniel K. Inouye was elected to the Senate and became a member of the Armed Services Committee and the Commerce Committee.

Spark Masayuki Matsunaga of Hawaii was elected to the seat in the House of Representatives that Daniel K. Inouye vacated and became a member of the Rules Committee.

Seiji Horiuchi was the first Nisei elected to a state legislature on the mainland, in Brighton, Colorado.

The JACL chose Minoru Yamasaki as Nisei of the Biennium. Among his many architectural accomplishments are the Century Plaza Hotel (Los Angeles), Japanese Cultural Trade Center (San Francisco), Municipal Air Terminal (St. Louis), Pacific Science Center (Seattle), and the Woodrow Wilson School for Public Affairs (Princeton). Yamasaki had received many other awards, including one for his design for the Oregon Capitol Building, and had been named by Time as one of the top ten architects of the United States. Others awarded by the JACL were Dr. Kiyo Tomiyasu, Tom Kitayama, Caesar Uyesaka, and John Yoshino.

1963   Wilfred C. Tsukiyama, chief justice of Hawaii, was awarded the Order of the Sacred Treasure Second Class by Japan for his contributions toward promotion of harmonious relations between the United States and Japan. It was the highest award ever presented to an American of Japanese ancestry.

Kotaro Suto, also known as "Papa Suto," died. He worked on Carl Fisher's estate in Miami Beach, Florida, but in his spare time, he planted (gratis) roses and trees everywhere in Miami Beach.

June 11. The House of Representatives set aside two hours to pay tribute to the Japanese-American military service in World War II. Twenty-four Congressmen spoke in tribute at a well-attended session.

1964   Patsy Takemoto Mink of Hawaii became the first Nisei woman elected to the House of Representatives.

Daniel K. Inouye seconded Lyndon Johnson's nomination at the Democratic National Convention in Atlantic City, New Jersey.

The JACL chose Henry Y. Kasai as Nisei of the Biennium. He was credited with encouraging the Utah legislature to eliminate many of its racist laws and in particular the one on miscegenation. Kasai had been cited by the Anti-Defamation League of B'nai B'rith and received the Americanism award from the Junior Chamber of Commerce. The JACL also recognized Dr. Thomas T. Omori and Rep. Spark Matsunaga for their respective contributions.

October 1. The final claim on the Japanese-American Evacuation Claim Act was adjudicated.

1965   President Lyndon Johnson signed the new immigration bill. This bill eliminated race, creed, and nationality as a basis for immigration; it based immigration on skills and on relationship to those already in the United States and limited the total number to enter to 350,000 per annum.

Larry Tajiri died. He was the drama editor of the Denver Post at the time of his death and his career as a newspaperman included California's Kashu Mainichi, the New York bureau of Tokyo's Asahi, and, very significantly, editor of the Pacific Citizen, the JACL newspaper.

October 8. A memorial for Kotaro "Papa" Suto was placed on the Miami Beach Conservatory.

1966   Rep. Patsy Takemoto Mink of Hawaii was reelected to Congress.

The JACL chose Rep. Patsy T. Mink of Hawaii as the Nisei of the Biennium. She was the first Nisei woman (1) in the U.S. House of Representatives, (2) in the state legislature of Hawaii, and (3) admitted to practice law in Hawaii. Others honored by the JACL were Kenji Fujii, Dr. Kazumi Kasuga, Yoshihiro Uchida, and Henry Ushijima.

The Japanese American Association was awarded the Golden Order of Merit Medallion by the Red Cross of Japan for their continued assistance during crises in Japan.

January 6. Chief Justice Wilfred C. Tsukiyama of Hawaii died. He had served the public in many posts since 1929.

1967   The California state legislature unanimously adopted Senate
             Resolution No. 101 wherein commendations and expressions
             of friendship and goodwill toward the Japanese Americans
             were cited.

             Daniel K. Inouye wrote an autobiography titled Journey to
             Washington.

1968   Senator Inouye introduced a bill to repeal Title II of the
             McCarran Act, otherwise known as the "detention camp"
             measure. The JACL was active in urging its repeal.

             Patsy Takemoto Mink was reelected to Congress. She be-
             came a member of the Education and Labor Committee and
             the Interior and Insular Affairs Committee.

             John F. Aiso was named justice for the California Court of
             Appeals by Gov. Ronald Reagan.

             San Francisco-born George F. Togasaki, first chairman of
             the board of Japan Christian University, became president
             of Rotary International for 1968-1969 and a Fellow of the
             University of California.

             Francis Takemoto retired as brigadier general of the U.S.
             Army Reserve.

             Grayson Taketa ran unsuccessfully for the state legislature
             from California's tenth district.

             Premier Eisaku Sato of Japan presented Mike Masaoka the
             Order of the Rising Sun, Third Class, one of the highest
             honors for foreigners.

             The JACL chose Norman Mineta, vice-mayor of San Jose,
             California, as Nisei of the Biennium for his community con-
             sciousness. Others honored were George Togasaki, David
             Furukawa, Dr. Chihiro Kikuchi, and Dr. Jin H. Kinoshita.

             The Buddhist Church of America named a Nisei for the first
             time as their bishop, the Reverend Kenryu T. Tsuji.

             Kosaku Sawada, a renowned grower and hybridizer of ca-
             mellias in Mobile, Alabama, died.

1969   Norman Y. Mineta was reelected city councilman and vice-mayor of San Jose, California. He was the first Nisei on the 117-year-old council.

The one hundredth anniversary of Japanese immigration to the United States was celebrated and President Nixon extended his greetings.

Bill Hosokawa wrote Nisei - The Quiet Americans, a history of the Japanese people in the United States.

October 21. Yoneo Arai was presented the Order of the Sacred Treasure, Third Class, by the Japanese government for contributing to the improvement of the United States-Japan relationships.

December 22. The U.S. Senate passed Daniel Inouye's bill to repeal Title II (the detention camp measure) of the Internal Security Act.

1970

Dr. Paul K. Kuroda received the Southwest Regional Award of the American Chemistry Society.

The JACL Nisei of the Biennium was Dr. Paul I. Terasaki in tissue immunology, who indirectly participated in Dr. Christian Barnard's first heart transplant. Also honored were Dr. S. I. Hayakawa, and Shiro Kashiwa, assistant district attorney, Washington, D.C.

Seiji Ozawa became conductor of the San Francisco Symphony Orchestra.

At a testimonial for Mike Masaoka in Chicago, a trust fund was established in his name and the first recipient of this award was Edwin O. Reischauer, professor at Harvard and former ambassador to Japan.

January 28. The National Leadership Conference on Civil Rights endorsed the JACL campaign to repeal Title II (detention camp measure) of the Internal Security Act.

March. 19. The New York garment workers held a one-day walk-out to protest imported clothing from the Far East.

March 24. Six JACL witnesses testified at the House Internal Security Committee hearing on the Title II repeal bill. Jerry Enomoto read Earl Warren's letter against Title II into the record.

Dr. Kenichi Nishimoto, Indian Health Service Administrator, was elected to the city council in Takoma Park, Maryland, thus becoming the first Nisei councilman on the East Coast.

April 7. Sgt. Rodney Yano of Hilo, Hawaii, was awarded the Medal of Honor posthumously by President Nixon. Sgt. Yano died on January 1, 1969, in Vietnam.

President Nixon signed imporant amendments to the 1965 Immigration Act.

June 22. The Voting Rights Act Amendment of 1970 eliminated the literacy test.

July 13. President Nixon signed an immigration bill to admit 205 Japanese residents of the Bonin Islands who claimed American sailors as their ancestors.

September 16. Harry I. Iseki, mayor of Parlier, California, died.

October 24. In New York the JACL honored Yoneo Arai, eighty years old, the oldest living Nisei in the United States, for his many contributions.

October 28. Kyoichi Sawada, a Pulitzer Prize-winning Issei photographer for the U.P.I., died in Cambodia while on assignment.

November 3. Representatives Spark Matsunaga and Patsy T. Mink, both of Hawaii, were reelected.

November 4. William Mo Marumoto was appointed a presidential assistant on executive manpower, becoming the first Nisei on the White House staff.

1971   Norman Y. Mineta was elected as mayor of San Jose, California.

Christy Ito joined the Ice Follies. She had received the Babbitt Award for five consecutive years (1967-1971).

Henry Hibino was elected councilman in Salinas, California.

Senator Daniel Inouye reintroduced the Title II repeal bill

(the detention camp measure) in the Senate. The previous bill had died when the House failed to act on it.

House Speaker Carl Albert paid tribute to Mike Masaoka on the House floor.

Congressmen Spark Matsunaga and Chet Holifield reintroduced their Title II repeal proposal (the detention camp measure) to the House.

Sculptor Isamu Noguchi was elected to the fifty-member American Academy of Arts and Letters in New York.

September. Shig Kariya became the first Nisei president of the Japanese American Association of New York.

September 23. President Nixon signed the Title II Repeal bill into Public Law 92-128.

December. Asian American delegates of the United States held a conference in Washington, D.C. with governmental representatives subsequent to not receiving any of the $32 million appropriated for the aged for 1969-71 period. The purpose of the conference was to call attention to the needs of Asian-American senior citizens.

December 13. The JACL drafted a bill to establish a cabinet committee on Asian Americans, which was introduced by Representatives Spark Matsunaga of Hawaii and Glenn M. Anderson of California in the House, along with twenty-three other cosponsors.

1972   Washington Governor Daniel J. Evans formed the Asian American Advisory Council consisting of twenty members.

The National Institute for Mental Health granted $320,000 to the Asian American Drug Abuse Program in Los Angeles.

The JACL honored Dr. Makio Murayama as Nisei of the Biennium. Dr. Murayama has been contributing as a researcher in sickle cell anemia at the National Institutes of Health in Bethesda, Maryland.

Joanne Mitsuko Funakoshi, an ice skater, toured Europe with the "Holiday on Ice" show.

January. Asian American groups protested the showing of Madame Sin, the ABC-TV movie of the week.

January 6. Shiro Kashiwa became the first American of Japanese ancestry appointed to a federal court as Associate Judge of the U.S. Court of Claims in Washington, D.C.

January 7. President Nixon met Prime Minister Eisaku Sato in San Clemente, California, and discussed the May 5 Okinawa reversion.

February. A U.S. District Court judge ruled the Georgia miscegenation law invalid.

March 22. Robert Kawaguchi died. He was a veteran of the 100th Infantry Battalion and served as Golden Gate VFW Post Commander in San Francisco.

April. Niseis who were elected in California municipal elections were Ken Nakaoka, mayor of Gardena; Paul Bannai, councilman of Gardena; Sak Yamamoto, councilman of Carson City; Dr. Tsujio Kato, councilman of Oxnard; Ken J. Nishio, councilman of Hemet City; Tom Kitayama (reelected) councilman of Union City; and S. Floyd Mori, councilman of Pleasanton.

Dr. Jin Kinoshita was appointed vision research director of the National Eye Institute in Bethesda, Maryland.

Michael Tadao Ito was named assistant district attorney in San Francisco.

May. Mike M. Suzuki was appointed director of children and family services with the Department of Health, Education and Welfare.

May 15. The treaty restoring the Ryukyu Islands (including Okinawa) to Japan formally ended the American occupation of Japan that began in 1945.

May 31. Harvey A. Itano, M.D., Ph.D., received the first Rev. Dr. Martin Luther King, Jr. Medical Achievement Award for Outstanding Contributions in Research of Sickle

Cell Anemia. It was presented by the Philadelphia chapter of the Southern Christian Leadership Conference.

June 8. Bill Hosokawa, associate editor of the Denver Post, represented the U.S. communications media at the United States-Japan Assembly in Shimoda, Japan.

July 12. Federal legislature repealed two anti-Oriental laws: the 1872 law prohibiting entry of Orientals without permit, and the 1905 law banning the import of an Oriental woman with intent to force her to live with someone or to sell her.

Kenzo Takada, a Paris designer from Japan, signed an agreement with the Asian American group in New York City to stop using the anti-Nisei label of JAP. Butterick Patterns subsequently removed the offensive name from their catalogs.

August 22. The ILGWU's "Don't Buy Made In Japan" posters were denounced by the Asian American group in New York and a request for their withdrawal was made.

September 5. The Social and Rehabilitation Service of the Department of Health, Education and Welfare funded five West Coast Asian American programs totalling $524,000.

September 19. NBC-TV televised Guilty by Reason of Race, a documentary about the Japanese American experience during World War II.

September 22. Construction began on the Air and Space Museum at the Smithsonian Institution, which was designed by Gyo Obata of St. Louis.

Mitsubishi of Japan donated $1 million to Harvard University for Japanese legal studies.

October 18. The White House hosted about fifty Asian American representatives.

October 25. The New York Asian American group picketed the ILGWU headquarters protesting the "racist" poster.

1973   Through a reinterpretation of the 1972 Social Security amendment, a number of Americans of Japanese ancestry became eligible for the special wage coverage for the World War II period.

Jena Minako Kobayashi became a member of the New Christy Minstrels, a singing and instrumental group.

The Federal Equal Employment Opportunity Commission awarded $61,000 to Asian, Inc., of San Francisco for research on job discrimination.

Paul T. Bannai of Salinas, California, was elected the first Nisei assemblyman.

In Salinas, California, Dr. Donald T. Hata, Jr. was named to fill the city council seat vacated by Paul T. Bannai, who was named to the state legislature.

David Ushio, national director of JACL, urged the prompt recall of offensive license plates bearing JAP or NIP combinations. Governor Ronald Reagan of California signed legislation authorizing the Department of Motor Vehicles to recall any offensive license plates.

The Japan Foundation of Japan contributed $10 million to ten universities in the United States to promote a deeper understanding of Japan and Japanese-American relations.

Senator Theodore Stevens of Alaska urged Japan to stop fishing for salmon due to diminished production.

Fortune magazine reported Japan as ranking top among the world's non-Communist nations in an annual rating report of non-United States manufacturing and banking corporations.

The Elks, the largest fraternal order in the United States, recommended the abolishment of their "whites-only" clause in their membership policy, ending the 105-year-old restriction.

The Sumitomo Bank of Japan contributed $2 million to Yale University.

Dr. Masato Hasegawa of Hawaii was the only Nisei of the three persons who received the Brotherhood Award presented by the Men's Club of the Temple Emanu-El in Honolulu.

Richard Yoshikawa became president of the San Joaquin
Delta College Board in California.

April. George Ise, a Nisei, was chosen mayor of Monterey
Park, California, by the city council.

May 2. Sak Yamamoto became mayor of Carson, Los Angeles county, through appointment by the city council.

July. Manken Toku Ishii died. He lived on a farm in Ker-
honkson, New York, and was dedicated to donating Japanese
cherry tree cuttings. Ishii was recognized and cited by
Mrs. Lyndon Johnson, as well as by the Emperor of Japan.
Oral Roberts University and many Catskill Mountain camps
were among the recipients of his cherry trees.

July. Dr. S.I. Hayakawa of California State University, San
Francisco, announced receipt of a $30,000 grant from Japan
for studies in United States-Japan relations.

July. The first Japanese-style hotel in New York opened on
Park Avenue. It was named the Kitano Hotel.

Dr. Kenneth N. Matsumura of the Immunity Research Laboratory was granted a patent for the world's first artificial
liver.

Stanley Uyehara was named deputy city attorney for Los Angeles.

July. In a post-Senate Watergate hearing interview, Attorney John J. Wilson was asked for his reaction to Committee
member Sen. Daniel Inouye's muttered remark of, "What
a liar" during the testimony of ex-Nixon aide John Ehrlich-
man. Wilson replied with a reference to Inouye as " . . .
that little Jap," which subsequently caused national reper-
cussions from those sensitive to any racial slurs.

July 6. Henry Hibino was elected mayor of Salinas, California.

July 18. Masashi Kawaguchi, president and owner of Fish-
king Processors, broke ground for a $3 million plant in Cali-
fornia.

August. The Boy Scouts of America apologized to the JACL

for the comedian Bob Hope, who used the racial slur "Jap" in a joke at the Jubilee's opening session in Seattle.

August 5. Thomas Kohachiro Takeshita died. He participated in the attempt to obtain naturalization for the Issei and was the author of Yamato Damashii Under the Stars and Stripes.

August 13. Attorney John J. Wilson wrote a letter to the Nichi Bei Times, a Japanese American newspaper in California, explaining that he was unaware of the derogatory connotation of the word "Jap."

August 18. The California legislature was lobbied to prevent further establishment of Japanese and other foreign-owned banks in California.

September 2-7. Dr. Roy H. Doi, a bacteriologist at the University of California - Davis, presented a paper at the First International Congress of Bacteriology in Jerusalem, Israel.

September 4. Alex Kimura became the first mainland person of Japanese ancestry to serve as a page in the U.S. Congress.

September 5. William Mo Marumoto, the highest-ranking Japanese American in the Nixon administration, resigned. He was responsible for recruitment of minority personnel on the cabinet and subcabinet level.

September 11. Dr. Tetsuo Akutsu, a pioneer in the development of artifical hearts, implanted one in a two-hundred-pound calf that survived for a record twenty-four days at the University of Mississippi Medical Center, Jackson, Mississippi.

Ruth H. Kodani of Los Angeles was named to the advisory board of the Automobile Club of Southern California. She was twice appointed to the President's Committee for Traffic Safety and formed the Women Leaders for Highway Safety.

October 23. Dr. Leo Esaki, an Issei in New York, received the Nobel Physics Prize for his electron tunneling theories.

JAPANESE IMMIGRATION -- THE GENTLEMEN'S AGREEMENT, 1908

Report of the Commissioner General of Immigration

The growing number of Japanese in California, and the hostility of labor to Oriental competition, led to an agitation against Japanese immigration that culminated in the San Francisco school laws of 1906. These laws required, in insulting terms, that Chinese, Japanese, and Korean children attend a separate Oriental Public School. The danger of further hostile legislation led President Roosevelt to conclude with Japan the famous Gentlemen's Agreement, -- an executive agreement, the exact terms of which have never been revealed. The agreement salved the pride of Japan, and temporarily placated the Californians. By permitting the immigration of wives, it increased the Japanese population in California materially, and was eventually superseded by the Immigration Act of 1924.

Source: By permission from Documents of American History, Vol. II, 8th Edition, edited by Henry Steele Commager, New York: Appleton-Century-Crofts, Educational Division, Meredith Corp., 1968.

In order that the best results might follow from an enforcement of the regulations, an understanding was reached with Japan that the existing policy of discouraging emigration of its subjects of the laboring classes to continental United States should be continued, and should, by co-operation with the governments, be made as effective as possible. This understanding contemplates that the Japanese government shall issue passports to continental United States only to such of its subjects as are non-laborers or are laborers who, in coming to the continent, seek to resume a formerly acquired domicile, to join a parent, wife, or children residing there, or to assume active control of an already possessed interest in a farming enterprise in this country, so that the three classes of laborers entitled to receive passports have come to be designated "former residents," "parents, wives, or children of residents," and "settled agriculturists."

With respect to Hawaii, the Japanese government of its own volition stated that, experimentally at least, the issuance of passports to members of the laboring classes proceeding thence would be limited to "former residents" and "parents, wives, or children of residents." The said government has also been exercising a careful supervision over the subject of emigration of its laboring class to foreign contiguous territory.

THE ROOT-TAKAHIRA AGREEMENT
November 30, 1908

This agreement was brought about by an exchange of notes between the Japanese Ambassador and Secretary of State Root. By it Japan apparently confirmed the Open Door policy in China, and both nations bound themselves to maintain the status quo in China. In as much as Japan had, in the preceding years, concluded a number of secret agreements with China and with Russia, giving to her exceptional privileges in China and Manchuria, the significance of the agreement is somewhat ambiguous.

Source: By permission from Documents of American History, Vol. II, 8th Edition, edited by Henry Steele Commager, New York: Appleton-Century-Crofts, Educational Division, Meredith Corp., 1968.

The Japanese Ambassador to the Secretary of State
        Imperial Japanese Embassy
        Washington, November 30, 1908
Sir: The exchange of views between us, which has taken place at the several interviews which I have recently had the honor of holding with you, has shown that Japan and the United States holding important outlying insular possessions in the region of the Pacific Ocean, the Governments of the two countries are animated by a common aim, policy, and intention in that region.

Believing that a frank avowal of that aim, policy, and intention would not only tend to strengthen the relations of friendship and good neighborhood, which have immemorially existed between Japan and the United States, but would materially contribute to the preservation of the general peace, the Imperial Government have authorized me to present to you an outline of their understanding of that common aim, policy and intention.

1. It is the wish of the two Governments to encourage the free and peaceful development of their commerce on the Pacific Ocean.

2. The policy of both Governments, uninfluenced by any aggressive tendencies, is directed to the maintenance of the existing status quo in the region above mentioned and to the defense of the principle of equal opportunity for commerce and industry in China.

3. They are accordingly firmly resolved reciprocally to respect the territorial possessions belonging to each other in said region.

4. They are also determined to preserve the common interest of all powers in China by supporting by all pacific means at their disposal the independence and integrity of China and the principle of equal opportunity for commerce and industry of all nations in that Empire.

5. Should any event occur threatening the status quo as above described or the principle of equal opportunity as above defined, it remains for the two Governments to communicate with each other in or-

der to arrive at an understanding as to what measures they may consider it useful to take.

If the foregoing outline accords with the view of the Government of the United States, I shall be gratified to receive your confirmation.

I take this opportunity to renew to your excellency the assurance of my highest consideration.

K. Takahira.

FINAL RECOMMENDATIONS OF THE COMMANDING GENERAL,
WESTERN DEFENSE COMMAND AND FOURTH ARMY,
SUBMITTED TO THE SECRETARY OF WAR
February 14, 1942

Headquarters Western Defense Command and Fourth Army
Presidio of San Francisco, California
Office of the Commanding General

February 14, 1942

014.31 (DCS)

Memorandum for: The Secretary of War
(Thru: The Commanding General,
Field Forces, Washington, D.C.)

Subject: Evacuation of Japanese and other Subversive Persons from the
Pacific Coast.

1. In presenting a recommendation for the evacuation of Japanese
and other subversive persons from the Pacific Coast, the following facts
have been considered:
    a. Mission of the Western Defense Command and Fourth Army.
        (1) Defense of the Pacific Coast of the Western Defense Com-
mand, as extended, against attacks by sea, land or air;
        (2) Local protection of establishment and communications vital
to the National Defense for which adequate defense cannot be provided
by local civilian authorities.
    b. Brief Estimate of the Situation.
        (1) Any estimate of the situation indicates that the following
are possible and probable enemy activities:
            (a) Naval attack on shipping in coastal waters;
            (b) Naval attack on coastal cities and vital installations;
            (c) Air raids on vital installations, particularly within two
                hundred miles of the coast;
            (d) Sabotage of vital installations throughout the Western De-
                fense Command.
    Hostile Naval and air raids will be assisted by enemy agents sig-
naling from the coastline and the vicinity thereof; and by supplying and
otherwise assisting enemy vessels and by sabotage.
    Sabotage, (for example, of airplane factories), may be effected not
only by destruction within plants and establishments, but by destroying
power, light, water, sewer and other utility and other facilities in the
immediate vicinity thereof or at a distance. Serious damage or destruction in congested areas may readily be caused by incendiarism.
        (2) The area lying to the west of the Cascade and Sierra

Nevada Mountains in Washington, Oregon and California, is highly cri-
ical not only because the lines of communication and supply to the
Pacific theater pass through it, but also because of the vital industrial
production therein, particularly aircraft. In the war in which we are
now engaged racial affinities are not severed by migration. The Japanese race is an enemy race and while many second and third genera-
tion Japanese born on United States soil, possessed of United States
citizenship, have become "Americanized," the racial strains are un-
diluted. To conclude otherwise is to expect that children born of white
parents on Japanese soil sever all racial affinity and become loyal Japanese subjects, ready to fight and, if necessary, to die for Japan in a
war against the nation of their parents. That Japan is allied with Germany
and Italy in this struggle is no ground for assuming that any Japanese,
barred from assimilation by convention as he is, though born and raised
in the United States, will not turn against this nation when the final test
of loyalty comes. It, therefore, follows that along the vital Pacific Coast
over 112,000 potential enemies, of Japanese extraction, are at large today. There are indications that these are organized and ready for con-
certed action at a favorable opportunity. The very fact that no sabotage
has taken place to date is a disturbing and confirming indication that
such action will be taken.

    c. Disposition of the Japanese.

        (1) Washington. As the term is used herein, the word "Jap-
anese" includes alien Japanese and American citizens of Japanese
ancestry. In the State of Washington the Japanese population, aggregating
over 14,500, is disposed largely in the area lying west of the Cascade
Mountains and south of an eastwest line passing through Bellingham,
Washington, about 70 miles north of Seattle and some 15 miles south of
the Canadian border. The largest concentration of Japanese is in the
area, the axis of which is along the line Seattle, Tacoma, Olympia,
Willapa Bay and the mouth of the Columbia River, with the heaviest
concentration in the agricultural valleys between Seattle and Tacoma,
viz., the Green River and the Puyallup Valleys. The Boeing Aircraft
factory is in the Green River Valley. The lines of communication and
supply including power and water which feed this vital industrial in-
stallation, radiate from this plant for many miles through areas heavily
populated by Japanese. Large numbers of Japanese also operate vegetable markets along the Seattle and Tacoma waterfronts, in Bremerton,
near the Bremerton Navy Yard, and inhabit islands in Puget Sound op-
posite vital naval ship building installations. Still others are engaged in
fishing along the southwest Washington Pacific Coast and along the
Columbia River. Many of these Japanese are within easy reach of the
forests of Washington State, the stock piles of seasoning lumber and
the many sawmills of southwest Washington. During the dry season
these forests, mills and stock piles are easily fired.

        (2) Oregon. There are approximately 4,000 Japanese in the
State of Oregon, of which the substantial majority reside in the area
in the vicinity of Portland along the south bank of the Columbia River,
following the general line Bonneville, Oregon City, Astoria, Tillamook,
Many of these are in the northern reaches of the Willamette Valley and

are engaged in agricultural and fishing pursuits. Others operate vegetable markets in the Portland metropolitan area and still others reside along the northern Oregon sea coast. Their disposition is in intimate relationship with the northwest Oregon sawmills and lumber industry, near and around the vital electric power development at Bonneville and the pulp and paper installations at Camas (on the Washington State side of the Columbia River) and Oregon City (directly south of Portland).

(3) California. The Japanese population in California aggregates approximately 93,500 people. Its disposition is so widespread and so well known that little would be gained by setting it forth in detail here. They live in great numbers along the coastal strip, in and around San Francisco and the Bay Area, the Salinas Valley, Los Angeles and San Diego. Their truck farms are contiguous to the vital aircraft industry concentration in and around Los Angeles. They live in large numbers in and about San Francisco, now a vast staging area for the war in the Pacific, a point at which the nation's lines of communication and supply converge. Inland they are disposed in the Sacramento, San Joaquin and Imperial Valleys. They are engaged in the production of approximately 38% of the vegetable produce of California. Many of them are engaged in the distribution of such produce in and along the waterfronts at San Francisco and Los Angeles. Of the 93,500 in California, about 25,000 reside inland in the mentioned valleys where they are largely engaged in vegetable production cited above, and 54,600 reside along the coastal strip, that is to say, a strip of coast line varying from eight miles in the north to twenty miles in width in and around the San Francisco bay area, including San Francisco, in Los Angeles and its environs, and in San Diego. Approximately 13,900 are dispersed throughout the remaining portion of the state. In Los Angeles City the disposition of vital aircraft industrial plants covers the entire city. Large numbers of Japanese live and operate markets and truck farms adjacent to or near these installations.

d. Disposition of Other Subversive Persons.

Disposed within the vital coastal strip already mentioned are large numbers of Italians and Germans, foreign and native born, among whom are many individuals who constitute an actual or potential menace to the safety of the nation.

2. Action recommended.

a. Recommendations for the designation of prohibited areas, described as "Category A" areas in California, Oregon and Washington, from which are to be excluded by order of the Attorney General all alien enemies, have gone forward from this headquarters to the Attorney General through the Provost Marshal General and the Secretary of War. These recommendations were made in order to aid the Attorney General in the implementation of the Presidential Proclamations of December 7 and 8, 1941, imposing responsibility on him for the control of alien enemies as such. These recommendations were for the exclusion of all alien enemies from Category "A." The Attorney General has adopted these recommendations in part, and has the balance under consideration. Similarly, recommendations were made by this headquarters, and adopted by the Attorney General, for the designation of certain areas as Category "B" areas, within which alien enemies may be permitted on pass or permit.

b. I now recommend the following:

(1) That the Secretary of War procure from the President direction and authority to designate military areas in the combat zone of the Western Theater of Operations, (if necessary to include the entire combat zone), from which, in his discretion, he may exclude all Japanese, all alien enemies, and all other persons suspected for any reason by the administering military authorities of being actual or potential saboteurs, espionage agents, or fifth columnists. Such executive order should empower the Secretary of War to requisition the services of any and all other agencies of the Federal Government, with express direction to such agencies to respond to such requisition, and further empowering the Secretary of War to use any and all federal facilities and equipment, including Civilian Conservation Corps Camps, and to accept the use of State facilities for the purpose of providing shelter and equipment for evacuees. Such executive order to provide further for the administration of military areas for the purposes of this plan by appropriate military authorities acting with the requisitioned assistance of the other federal agencies and the cooperation of State and local agencies. The executive order should further provide that by reason of military necessity the right of all persons, whether citizens or aliens, to reside, enter, cross or be within any military areas shall be subject to revocation and shall exist on a pass and permit basis at the discretion of the Secretary of War and implemented by the necessary legislation imposing penalties for violation.

(2) That, pursuant to such executive order, there be designated as military areas all areas in Washington, Oregon and California, recommended by me to date for designation by the Attorney General as Category "A" areas and such additional areas as it may be found necessary to designate hereafter.

(3) That the Secretary of War provide for the exclusion from such military areas, in his discretion, of the following classes of persons, viz:

(a) Japanese aliens.

(b) Japanese-American citizens.

(c) Alien enemies other than Japanese aliens.

(d) Any and all other persons who are suspected for any reason by the administering military authorities to be actual or potential saboteurs, espionage agents, fifth columnists, or subversive persons.

(4) That the evacuation of classes (a), (b), and (c) from such military areas be initiated on a designated evacuation day and carried to completion as rapidly as practicable.

That prior to evacuation day all plans be complete for the establishment of initial concentration points, reception centers, registration, rationing, guarding, transportation to internment points, and the selection and establishment of internment facilities in the Sixth, Seventh, and Eighth Corps Areas.

That persons in class (a) and (c) above be evacuated and

interned at such selected places of internment, under guard.

That persons in class (b) above, at the time of evacuation, be offered an opportunity to accept voluntary internment, under guard, at the place of internment above mentioned.

That persons in class (b) who decline to accept voluntary internment, be excluded from all military areas, and left to their own resources, or, in the alternative, be encouraged to accept resettlement outside of such military areas with such assistance as the State governments concerned or the Federal Security Agency may be by that time prepared to offer.

That the evacuation of persons in class (d) be progressive and continuing, and that upon their evacuation persons in class (d) be excluded from all military areas and left in their own resources outside of such military areas, or, in the alternative, be offered voluntary internment or encouraged to accept voluntary resettlement as above outlined, unless the facts in a particular case shall warrant other action.

(5) The Commanding General, Western Defense Command and Fourth Army, to be responsible for the evacuation, administration, supply and guard, to the place of internment; the Commanding Generals of the Corps Areas concerned to be responsible for guard, supply and administration at the places of internment.

(6) That direct communication between the Commanding General, Western Defense Command and Fourth Army and the Corps Area Commanders concerned for the purpose of making necessary arrangements be authorized.

(7) That the Provost Marshal General coordinate all phases of the plan between the Commanding General, Western Defense Command and Fourth Army, on the one hand, and the Corps Area Commanders on the other hand.

(8) That all arrangements be accomplished with the utmost secrecy.

(9) That adult males (above the age of 14 years) be interned separately from all women and children until the establishment of family units can be accomplished.

(10) No change is contemplated in Category "B" areas.

3. Although so far as the Army is concerned, such action is not an essential feature of the plan, but merely incident thereto, I, nevertheless, recommend that mass internment be considered as largely a temporary expedient pending selective resettlement, to be accomplished by the various Security Agencies of the Federal and State Governments.

4. The number of persons involved in the recommended evacuation will be approximately 133,000. (This total represents all enemy aliens and Japanese-American citizens in Category "A" areas recommended to date.)

5. If these recommendations are approved detailed plans will be made by this headquarters for the proposed evacuation. The number evacuated to be apportioned by the Provost Marshal General among the Corps Area Commanders concerned as the basis for formulating their respective plans. It is possible that the State of California, and perhaps the State of Washington, will be able to offer resettlement facilities for

a given number of evacuees who may be willing to accept resettlement.

6. Pending further and detailed study of the problem, it is further recommended: (1) That the Commanding General, Western Defense Command and Fourth Army, coordinate with the local and State authorities, in order to facilitate the temporary physical protection by them of the property of evacuees not taken with them; (2) That the Commanding General, Western Defense Command and Fourth Army, determine the quantity and character of property which the adult males, referred to in paragraph 2b (9), may be permitted to take with them; and (3) That the Treasury Department or other proper Federal agency be responsible for the conservation, liquidation, and proper disposition of the property of evacuees if it cannot be cared for through the usual and normal channels.

J. L. DeWitt
Lieutenant General, U.S. Army,
Commanding.

EXECUTIVE ORDER NO. 9066
February 19, 1942

Authorizing the Secretary of War to Prescribe
Military Areas

Whereas, The successful prosecution of the war requires every possible protection against espionage and against sabotage to national-defense
material, national-defense premises and national-defense utilities as defined in Section 4, Act of April 20, 1918, 40 Stat. 533, as amended by the
Act of November 30, 1940, 54 Stat. 1220, and the Act of August 21, 1941,
55 Stat. 655 (U.S.C., Title 50, Sec. 104):

Now, therefore, by virtue of the authority vested in me as President
of the United States, and Commander in Chief of the Army and Navy, I hereby authorized and direct the Secretary of War, and the Military Commanders whom he may from time to time designate, whenever he or any designated Commander deems such action necessary or desirable, to prescribe
military areas in such places and of such extent as he or the appropriate
Military Commander may determine, from which any or all persons may
be excluded, and with respect to which, the right of any person to enter,
remain in, or leave shall be subject to whatever restriction the Secretary
of War or the appropriate Military Commander may impose in his discretion. The Secretary of War is hereby authorized to provide for residents
of any such area who are excluded therefrom, such transportation, food,
shelter, and other accommodations as may be necessary, in the judgment
of the Secretary of War or the said Military Commander, and until other
arrangements are made, to accomplish the purpose of this order. The
designation of military areas in any region or locality shall supersede des-
ignations of prohibited and restricted areas by the Attorney General under
the Proclamation of December 7 and 8, 1941, and shall supersede the responsibility and authority of the Attorney General under the said Proclamations in respect of such prohibited and restricted areas.

I hereby further authorize and direct the Secretary of War and the said
Military Commanders to take such other steps as he or the appropriate
Military Commander may deem advisable to enforce compliance with the
restrictions applicable to each Military area hereinabove authorized to be
designated, including the use of Federal troops and other Federal Agencies,
with authority to accept assistance of state and local agencies.

I hereby further authorize and direct all Executive Departments, independent establishments and other Federal Agencies, to assist the Secretary
of War or the said Military Commanders in carrying out this Executive Order, including the furnishing of medical aid, hospitalization, food, clothing,
transportation, use of land, shelter, and other supplies, equipment, utilities, facilities, and services.

This order shall not be construed as modifying or limiting in any way the authority heretofore granted under Executive Order No. 8972, dated December 12, 1941, nor shall it be construed as limiting or modifying the duty and responsibility of the Federal Bureau of Investigation, with respect to the investigations of alleged acts of sabotage or the duty and responsibility of the Attorney General and the Department of Justice under the Proclamations of December 7 and 8, 1941, prescribing regulations for the conduct and control of alien enemies, except as such duty and responsibility is superseded by the designation of military areas hereunder.

Franklin D. Roosevelt

The White House, February 19, 1942.

EXECUTIVE ORDER NO. 9102
March 18, 1942

Establishing the War Relocation Authority in the Executive
Office of the President and Defining Its Functions and Duties

Dated March 18, 1942
7 F. R. 2165

By virtue of the authority vested in me by the Constitution and statutes
of the United States, as President of the United States and Commander in
Chief of the Army and Navy, and in order to provide for the removal from
designated areas of persons whose removal is necessary in the interests
of national security, it is ordered as follows:

1. There is established in the Office for Emergency Management of
the Executive Office of the President the War Relocation Authority, at the
head of which shall be a Director appointed by and responsible to the President.

2. The Director of the War Relocation Authority is authorized and directed to formulate and effectuate a program for the removal, from areas
designated from time to time by the Secretary of War or appropriate military commander under the authority of Executive Order No. 9066 of February 19, 1942, of the persons or classes of persons designated under such
Executive Order, and for their relocation, maintenance, and supervision.

3. In effectuating such program the Director shall have authority to:

(a) Accomplish all necessary evacuation not undertaken by the
Secretary of War or appropriate military commander, provide for the relocation of such persons in appropriate places, provide for their needs in
such manner as may be appropriate, and supervise their activities.

(b) Provide, insofar as feasible and desirable, for the employment of such persons at useful work in industry, commerce, agriculture,
or public projects, prescribe the terms and conditions of such public employment, and safeguard the public interest in the private employment of
such persons.

(c) Secure the cooperation, assistance, or services of any governmental agency.

(d) Prescribe regulations necessary or desirable to promote effective execution of such program, and, as a means of coordinating evacuation
and relocation activities, consult with the Secretary of War with respect to
regulations issued and measures taken by him.

(e) Make such delegations of authority as he may deem necessary.

(f) Employ necessary personnel, and make such expenditures, including the making of loans and grants and the purchase of real property,
as may be necessary, within the limits of such funds as may be made available to the Authority.

4. The Director shall consult with the United States Employment Service and other agencies on employment and other problems incident to activities under this order.

5. The Director shall cooperate with the Alien Property Custodian appointed pursuant to Executive Order No. 9095 of March 11, 1942, in formulating policies to govern the custody, management, and disposal by the Alien Property Custodian of property belonging to foreign nationals removed under this order or under Executive Order No. 9066 of February 19, 1942; and may assist all other persons removed under either of such Executive Orders in the management and disposal of their property.

6. Departments and agencies of the United States are directed to cooperate with and assist the Director in his activities hereunder. The Departments of War and Justice, under the direction of the Secretary of War and the Attorney General, respectively, shall insofar as consistent with national interest provide such protective, police and investigational services as the Director shall find necessary in connection with activities under this order.

7. There is established within the War Relocation Authority the War Relocation Work Corps. The Director shall provide, by general regulations, for the enlistment in such Corps, for the duration of the present war, of persons removed under this order or under Executive Order No. 9066 of February 19, 1942, and shall prescribe the terms and conditions of the work to be performed by such Corps, and the compensation to be paid.

8. There is established within the War Relocation Authority a Liaison Committee on War Relocation which shall consist of the Secretary of War, the Secretary of the Treasury, the Attorney General, the Secretary of Agriculture, the Secretary of Labor, the Federal Security Administrator, the Director of Civilian Defense, and the Alien Property Custodian, or their deputies, and such other persons or agencies as the Director may designate. The Liaison Committee shall meet at the call of the Director and shall assist him in his duties.

9. The Director shall keep the President informed with regard to the progress made in carrying out this order, and perform such related duties as the President may from time to time assign to him.

10. In order to avoid duplication of evacuation activities under this order and Executive Order No. 9066 of February 19, 1942, the Director shall not undertake any evacuation activities within military areas designated under said Executive Order No. 9066, without the prior approval of the Secretary of War or the appropriate military commander.

11. This order does not limit the authority granted in Executive Order No. 8972 of December 12, 1941; Executive Order No. 9066 of February 19, 1942; Executive Order No. 9095 of March 11, 1942; Executive Proclamation No. 2525 of December 7, 1941; Executive Proclamation No. 2526 of December 8, 1941; Executive Proclamation No. 2527 of December 8, 1941; Executive Proclamation No. 2533 of December 29, 1941; or Executive Proclamation No. 2537 of January 14, 1942; nor does it limit the functions of the Federal Bureau of Investigation.

PUBLIC LAW NO. 503 (77TH CONGRESS)
March 21, 1942

Dated March 21, 1942

To provide a penalty for violation of restrictions or orders with respect to persons entering, remaining in, leaving, or committing any act in military areas or zones.

Be it enacted by the Senate and House of Representatives of the United States of America in Congress assembled, That whoever shall enter, remain in, leave, or commit any act in any military area or military zone prescribed, under the authority of an Executive order of the President, by the Secretary of War, contrary to the restrictions applicable to any such area or zone or contrary to the order of the Secretary of War or any such military commander, shall, if it appears that he knew or should have known of the existence and extent of the restrictions or order and that his act was in violation thereof, be guilty of misdemeanor and upon conviction shall be liable to a fine of not to exceed $5,000 or to imprisonment for not more than one year, or both, for each offense.

CIVILIAN EXCLUSION ORDER NO. 5

Western Defense Command and Fourth Army
Wartime Civil Control Administration

Presidio of San Francisco, California
April 1, 1942

INSTRUCTIONS
to All Persons of
Japanese
Ancestry
Living in the Following Area:

All that portion of the City and County of San Francisco, State of California, lying generally west of the north-south line established by Junipero Serra Boulevard, Worchester Avenue, and Nineteenth Avenue, and lying generally north of the east-west line established by California Street, to the intersection of Market Street, and thence on Market Street to San Francisco Bay.

All Japanese persons, both alien and non-alien, will be evacuated from the above designated area by 12:00 o'clock noon, Tuesday, April 7, 1942.

No Japanese person will be permitted to enter or leave the above described area after 8:00 a.m., Thursday, April 2, 1942, without obtaining special permission from the Provost Marshal at the Civil Control Station located at:

1701 Van Ness Avenue
San Francisco, California

The Civil Control Station is equipped to assist the Japanese population affected by this evacuation in the following ways:

1. Give advice and instructions on the evacuation.

2. Provide services with respect to the management, leasing, sale, storage or other disposition of most kinds of property including: real estate, business and professional equipment, buildings, household goods, boats, automobiles, livestock, etc.

3. Provide temporary residence elsewhere for all Japanese in family groups.

4. Transport persons and a limited amount of clothing and equipment to their new residence, as specified below.

THE FOLLOWING INSTRUCTIONS MUST BE OBSERVED:

1. A responsible member of each family, preferably the head of the family, or the person in whose name most of the property is held, and each

individual living alone, will report to the Civil Control Station to receive further instructions. This must be done between 8:00 a.m. and 5:00 p.m., Thursday, April 2, 1942, or between 8:00 a.m. and 5:00 p.m., Friday, April 3, 1942.

2. Evacuees must carry with them on departure for the Reception Center, the following property:

(a) Bedding and linens (no mattress) for each member of the family;

(b) Toilet articles for each member of the family;

(c) Extra clothing for each member of the family;

(d) Sufficient knives, forks, spoons, plates, bowls and cups for each member of the family;

(e) Essential personal effects for each member of the family.

All items carried will be securely packaged, tied and plainly marked with the name of the owner and numbered in accordance with instructions received at the Civil Control Station.

The Size and number of packages is limited to that which can be carried by the individual or family group.

No contraband items as described in paragraph 6, Public Proclamation No. 3, Headquarters Western Defense Command and Fourth Army, dated March 24, 1942, will be carried.

3. The United States Government through its agencies will provide for the storage at the sole risk of the owner of the more substantial household items, such as iceboxes, washing machines, pianos and other heavy furniture. Cooking utensils and other small items will be accepted if crated, packed and plainly marked with the name and address of the owner. Only one name and address will be used by a given family.

4. Each family, and individual living alone, will be furnished transportation to the Reception Center. Private means of transportation will not be utilized. All instructions pertaining to the movement will be obtained at the Civil Control Station.

Go to the Civil Control Station at 1701 Van Ness Avenue, San Francisco, California, between 8:00 a.m. and 5:00 p.m., Thursday, April 2, 1942, or between 8:00 a.m. and 5:00 p.m., Friday, April 3, 1942, to receive further instructions.

J.L. DeWITT
Lieutenant General, U.S. Army
Commanding

PRESIDENT ROOSEVELT'S LETTER OF APPROVAL REGARDING
PROPOSED JAPANESE AMERICAN COMBAT TEAM
February 1, 1943

THE WHITE HOUSE

February 1, 1943

My Dear Mr. Secretary:

The proposal of the War Department to organize a combat team consisting of loyal American citizens of Japanese descent has my full approval. The new combat team will add to the nearly 5,000 loyal Americans of Japanese ancestry who are already serving in the armed forces of our country.

This is a natural and logical step towards the reinstitution of the Selective Service procedures which were temporarily disrupted by the evacuation from the West Coast.

No loyal citizen of the United States should be denied the democratic right to exercise the responsibilities of citizenship, regardless of his ancestry.   The principle on which this country was founded and by which it has always been governed is that Americanism is a matter of the mind and heart; Americanism is not, and never was, a matter of race or ancestry. A good American is one who is loyal to this country and to our creed of liberty and democracy. Every loyal American citizen should be given the opportunity to serve this country wherever his skills will make the greatest contribution -- whether it be in the ranks of the armed forces, war production, agriculture, government service, or other work essential to the war effort.

I am glad to observe that the War Department, the Navy Department, the War Manpower Commission, the Department of Justice, and the War Relocation Authority are collaborating in a program which will insure the opportunity for all loyal Americans, including Americans of Japanese ancestry, to serve their country at a time when the fullest and wisest use of our manpower is all important to the war effort.

Very sincerely yours,

/s/ Franklin D. Roosevelt

WRA REPORT OF THE TULE LAKE INCIDENT

Source: By permission from Uprooted Americans: Japanese Americans and the War Relocation Authority During World War II, Dillon S. Myer, Tucson: University of Arizona Press, copyright 1971.

Office of War Information, War Relocation Authority
The Tule Lake Incident
November 14, 1943

November 14, 1943

Dillon S. Myer, Director of the War Relocation Authority, today issued the following statement regarding the events that occurred between November 1 and November 4 at the Tule Lake Center in northern California:

1. Tule Lake is the only center maintained by the War Relocation Authority for segregation purposes. It was established originally in 1942 as one of 10 relocation centers for persons of Japanese ancestry who were evacuated from the West Coast military area. In September of this year, however, it was made the focal point in a segregation program carried out by the War Relocation Authority and since that time has occupied a peculiar status among WRA centers.

During February and March of this year, a registration program was conducted at all relocation centers for the purpose of accumulating information on the background and attitudes of all adult residents. As part of this program, citizen evacuees at the centers were questioned concerning their allegiance to the United States, and alien evacuees were questioned about their willingness to abide by the Nation's laws. After the results of registration were compiled and analyzed, WRA began a program to separate from the bulk of the population at relocation centers, those evacuees who have indicated by word or action that their loyalties lie with Japan.

Four major groups were designated for segregation:

(1) Those who requested repatriation or expatriation to Japan;

(2) Citizens who refused during registration to state unqualified allegiance to the United States and aliens who refused to agree to abide by the laws of the United States;

(3) Those with intelligence records or other records indicating that they might endanger the national security or interfere with the war effort;

(4) Close relatives of persons in the above three groups who expressed a preference to remain with the segregants rather than disrupt family ties.

The major movement of segregants into Tule Lake from other WRA centers and of non-segregants from Tule Lake to other WRA centers was started in early September and completed about the middle of October.

The process, which was carried out jointly with WRA and the Army, entirely without incident, involved the movement of approximately 9,000 evacuees from other centers into Tule Lake and the removal from Tule Lake to other centers of approximately the same number. Slightly more than 6,000 residents of Tule Lake who had been designated for segregation or who wished to remain with segregated relatives were retained there. At the present time, there are at the Manzanar Relocation Center in California approximately 1,900 evacuees who are awaiting transfer to Tule Lake. They will be transferred as soon as necessary housing can be completed, probably in the early part of 1944.

2. The Army has the responsibility of providing full protection of the area surrounding the Tule Lake Center. A man-proof fence surrounds the external boundaries of the center; troops patrol that fence; other necessary facilities are at all times in readiness. In September, when Tule Lake was transformed into a segregation center, the Army substantially increased the number of troops assigned to guard duty at the center and built the present man-proof fence around the external boundary outside the ordinary wire fence which was erected at the time of the center's establishment. At this time also additional military equipment was provided.

During the recent disturbance at the Tule Lake Center, the War Relocation Authority and the Army have been in constant contact regarding necessary safety measures. Special arrangements were made for prompt communication between the WRA staff and the officer commanding the troops at Tule Lake.

Like all WRA centers, Tule Lake has been operated, ever since the time of its establishment in 1942, under the terms of an agreement between WRA and the War Department. WRA is responsible for all phases of internal administration of the center. The Army, from the beginning, has been responsible for guarding the external boundaries of the center, and for controlling the entry and departure of all persons of Japanese descent.

WRA maintains order within the center through civilian guards assisted by a staff of evacuees. The understanding with the Army provides that when a show of greater force is necessary to maintain order within the center, WRA will call upon the Army to move inside the center and take full control.

3. Immediately following the segregation movement, some of the evacuees at the Tule Lake Center began to create difficulties. All available evidence indicates that a small, well-organized group -- composed chiefly of persons transferred to Tule Lake from the other centers -- was attempting to gain control of the community and disrupt the orderly process of administration. Against this background, a serious accident occurred at the center on October 15. A truck, carrying 29 evacuee workers and driven by an evacuee, was overturned while attempting to pass another truck on the road from the center to the WRA farm. All occupants of the truck were injured and one of them subsequently died. On the day following the accident, no evacuee workers reported for duty at the farm.

For a period of approximately 10 days thereafter, work on the harvesting of crops stopped, but no formal representations were made to WRA by evacuee workers. Then on October 25, a group of evacuees who claimed to represent the community met with Project Director Ray Best and submitted a series of questions and demands. Among other things, this committee asked whether the residents of Tule were regarded by the United States government as prisoners of war and stated that the residents would not engage in the harvesting of crops for use at other WRA centers. Project Director Best told the committee: (1) that the residents of Tule Lake were regarded as segregants and not as prisoners of war, (2) that WRA does not operate on the basis of demands, and (3) that if the residents of Tule Lake were unwilling to harvest the crops, some other method of harvesting them would be found.

Faced with the onset of winter and the possibility of losing approximately $500,000 worth of vegetables, WRA immediately began recruiting loyal evacuees from other centers to carry out the harvesting work at Tule Lake. A crew of 234 was recruited and is still engaged in harvesting work on the Tule Lake farm. These evacuees are quartered outside the boundaries of the center, wholly apart from the population of the center.

4. On the morning of Monday, November 1, D.S. Myer, National Director of the War Relocation Authority, and Robert B. Cozzens, Assistant Director of the Authority in San Francisco, arrived at the Tule Lake center for an inspection and consultation with key WRA staff members and with evacuee representatives. The original arrangement called for Mr. Myer and Mr. Cozzens to meet with evacuee representatives on the day following their arrival. However, during the lunch hour, a report was received by Project Director Best that certain evacuees were making unauthorized announcements in the evacuee mess halls. Residents were being told, according to this report, that Mr. Myer was to make a speech from the main administration building shortly after lunch. On receiving this report, Mr. Myer and Mr. Best immediately made a quick automobile inspection trip through the evacuee section of the center. They observed that large numbers of men, women and children were proceeding in an orderly manner from the evacuee barracks in the direction of the administration building.

By 1:30 p.m., Mr. Myer and Mr. Best had returned to the administration building and a crowd estimated between 3,500 and 4,000 had congregated immediately outside. One young man from the evacuee group then entered the administration building and asked whether a committee of 17 evacuees might have a conference with Mr. Myer. This request was granted and Mr. Myer, Mr. Cozzens, Mr. Best and other staff members met with the committee. The commitee presented a series of demands including the resignation of project director Best and several other WRA staff members at the center.

While the discussion was going on, word was received that a group of about a dozen evacuees had entered a center hospital and beaten the Chief Medical Officer, Dr. Reece M. Pedicord. The conference was interrupted while one WRA staff member left the administration building, passed through the crowd, and went to the hospital for a check-up on the situation there. After this man had returned -- wholly unmolested -- with the report that Dr. Pedicord had been badly battered but was receiving adequate medical attention and that order prevailed in the hospital, the conference was resumed. Meanwhile, a small group of evacuees had gone into the administration building and installed a public address system with WRA permission.

At the conclusion of the conference, Director Myer was asked to address the crowd briefly over the address system and agreed to do so. Mr. Myer told the crowd substantially what he told the committee: (1) that WRA would consider requests made by the evacuee population provided they were in the framework of national policy; (2) that WRA would not accede to demands; (3) that WRA was under the impression that the majority of residents at Tule Lake wanted to live in a peaceful and orderly atmosphere; (4) that if the residents of the center could not deal peacefully with WRA they would have to deal with someone else; and (5) that once the segregation process was wholly completed with the movement from Manzanar, the community at Tule Lake should attempt to select a committee -- more directly representative of its wishes than the current one -- to deal with the War Relocation Authority. After Mr. Myer had concluded his remarks, two members of the evacuee committee addressed the crowd briefly in Japanese. Immediately following the completion of these speeches, at about 4:30 p.m., the crowd broke up quickly and peacefully and returned to family living quarters. During the entire conference and the time when committee members were addressing the crowd, a member of the War Relocation Authority staff who is fully competent in the Japanese language was present and was able to indicate to Mr. Myer and Mr. Best the nature of all remarks made in Japanese.

5. While the meeting was in progress in the administration building a number of automobiles at the center were slightly damaged. Some of these automobiles belonged to visitors and some to WRA personnel. One visitor reported that a window of his car was broken and a sun visor removed. (This statement has not been verified by other evidence.) A door handle was broken off one car. Radio aerials were removed from two cars and windshield wipers from about twelve cars. Air was released from tires of several cars. The paint on two cars was scratched.

In the struggle during which Dr. Pedicord was beaten, a wooden railing in the hospital office was knocked down. A careful investigation has revealed no reliable evidence of any property damage during this incident other than that listed here.

Several WRA employees and visitors to the center who were in the area outside the administration building at the time the crowd was forming were approached by some of the evacuees directing the movements of the crowd and told to go inside the building. Aside from Dr. Pedicord, however, no WRA employees or visitors were beaten or injured during this incident. The evacuee employees in the administration office left their work. A few individuals reported they saw knives and clubs in the hands of some of the evacuees. The great majority of WRA personnel reported following the meeting that they had seen no weapons of any kind.

6. After dispersal of the crowd on Monday afternoon, a calm marked by some evidence of sub-surface tension prevailed in the evacuee community for approximately three days. Orders were sent out following the Monday meeting forbidding any meetings or assembly of evacuees in the administrative area. The internal security force was strengthened and authority was given for any member of the internal security staff, under certain specified conditions, to summon the Army directly without consultation with the Project Director or any other superior officer.

On Thursday afternoon, November 4, work was started on a fence separating the evacuee community from the section of the center where the administrative buildings are located and WRA staff members are housed. That evening a crowd of about 400 evacuees, mainly young men -- many of them armed with clubs -- entered the administration area. Most of the crowd entered the warehouse area. A few entered the motor pool area and some surrounded the Project Director's residence. The advance of this crowd was resisted by several WRA internal security officers, one of whom tripped, struck his head on a stone, and was then struck by evacuees with clubs. No other persons were injured. As the crowd closed in around Mr. Best's home, he telephoned Lt. Col. Verne Austin, commanding officer of the military unit outside the center, and asked the Army to assume full control of the project area. Troops entered the center at once.

7. During and immediately following the evacuee meeting on Monday, a number of the WRA staff became apprehensive concerning their personal safety. Most of them remained calm but a few became almost hysterical. All were offered the opportunity to leave the center until they felt secure in returning there, and a number of them did so. Since the incident on Monday, twelve people have resigned voluntarily, and two have resigned or were separated at the request of the Authority.

8. A large number of the evacuees at Tule Lake are citizens of the United States, with the constitutional rights of citizens. Many of them are children under 17, and they, together with a very large number of the adults, have no responsible part in the recent events.

In presenting this factual statement, the War Relocation Authority wants to emphasize that reports of the events at Tule Lake are being watched in Tokyo. Already some of the recent newspaper accounts have been used by the Japanese Government for propaganda purposes. There is every possibility that they may be used as a pretext for retaliatory action against American civilians and prisoners of war under Japanese control. Under these circumstances, it is imperative that the situation at Tule Lake be handled with a scrupulous regard for accuracy.

9. In view of the serious international implications in the situation at Tule Lake, the War Relocation Authority has been particularly careful in preparing the information contained in this statement. There have been so

many exaggerated, even hysterical, reports that the staff at Tule Lake, con-fronted with an otherwise complicated and difficult situation, has been able to verify conclusively only the information presented in this statement. As this is written, further investigation is being made to check the accuracy of many of the allegations that have appeared in the press and to complete this story in all its pertinent details. The major events, however, have now been fully documented and can for the first time be presented to the public in an official statement.

MEMORANDUM TO SECRETARY HAROLD ICKES FOLLOWING WRA
TRANSFER TO THE DEPARTMENT OF THE INTERIOR
February 29, 1944

Source: By permission from Uprooted Americans: Japanese Americans
and the War Relocation Authority During World War II, Dillon S. Myer,
Tucson: University of Arizona Press, copyright 1971.

Subject: Major Problems of the War Relocation Authority -- Past,
Present, and Future

Dear Mr. Ickes:

This memorandum is an attempt to outline for you some of the problems
of the War Relocation Authority, a summary of the present status, and a
brief outline of problems ahead as we now see them.

In general the problems with which we have had to deal in the past have
been divided into six major groups:

1. Recruitment, training, and maintenance of a staff for ten relocation centers, other field offices, and the Washington office.

It was a major task to locate personnel during the spring and summer
of 1942 to administer ten cities ranging in size from 7,000 to 17,500. Each
of these cities had most of the problems of any normal city of similar size
with some additional ones which a normal city does not have. It was necessary to provide at each center a school system, sanitary facilities, fire department, police department, and other services. In addition it was necessary to supply medical service and hospitals for the total population, provide transporation, supplies, and facilities for feeding the total population
in mess halls, which included problems with which the Army never had to
deal because they handle only men whereas we had men, women, and children. Special provisions had to be worked out for the organization of community enterprises such as stores, barber shops, shoe shops, etc., because of the unusual situation existing in each center. A wholly new type
of governmental structure was required, including provisions for courts,
community representation in administration, and special arrangements for
community activities, all of which had to be considered in the recruitment,
selection, and training of personnel. This basic job was only well under
way when it became necessary to establish property offices up and down the
West Coast in order to render service to the evacuees in relation to both
personal and real property, and immediately following that it became necessary to establish field offices at approximately fifty points throughout
the country in order to facilitate the relocation program.

Living conditions in relocation centers have been primitive and highly
undesirable, particularly during the early months of center existence. Be-

cause of the emotions involved it was necessary to select with care all the individuals employed, not only with respect to their professional competence but also their feelings about racial minorities and, particularly, any prejudices which might affect their ability to get along with evacuees.

2. The formulation of policies and procedures relating to the operation of the centers, and attendant problems.

Certain decisions had to be made very early in the program in order to present a budget to the Congress and to effect the framework of an organization. Because the job to be done was without precedent, many of the policies and procedures could not be established until a certain amount of experience had been gained by the Authority. Consequently, the major policies relating to administration were not drafted in detail until late August, 1942. It became essential then to take time out to draft policies needed to give guidance to the various centers. A major portion of these basic policies were put into effect during late August and early September of 1942. They have been continually revised and augmented since that time. They had to be drafted with care so that they would be acceptable to the public and the Congress and at the same time be acceptable to the evacuees so that orderly administration could be established within the relocation centers. Every step had to be reasoned through from the standpoint of both the general public and the evacuees, and reasons why each of the policies was established had to be sound and clear-cut.

3. The formulation and execution of relocation and segregation policies and procedures.

The formulation of policies relating to relocation outside the centers and the consideration of the segregation problem started almost immediately after the inception of the Authority. Seasonal leave policies were worked out with the War Department during May, 1942. The first indefinite leave regulation was issued on July 20, 1942. Leave procedures were reconsidered in August and September and were revised effective October 1, 1942. Here again it was necessary to keep in mind the problem of securing public and evacuee acceptance and to lay the ground work for more detailed procedures to be developed over a period of time providing for leave clearance or ultimate segregation of evacuees to a segregation center. These policies have had to be revised from time to time to meet new problems which have developed as relocation proceeded. Only recently we have revised the seasonal leave program in order to meet the present day problems.

The problem of securing information regarding each individual and family which would provide the background necessary for proper placement outside of relocation centers and employment within the centers, and provide basic information which would assist in the segregation process, was one of the most difficult ones we have had to handle. With the announcement by the Secretary of War of plans to organize a Japanese American combat team in January of 1943, procedures were worked out jointly by representatives of the Army, Navy, and the War Relocation Authority to register everyone in the centers 17 years of age and over, both citizens and aliens, using a questionnaire developed with the Office of Naval Intelligence and other agencies, and including the now famous questions 27 and 28 relating to willingness to serve in the United States Army and allegiance to the United States. Following the completion of the registration program steps were taken immediately in collaboration with the Japanese American Joint Board to complete the leave clearance procedures and determine which evacuees should be denied leave clearance. The information secured on these registration forms was supplemented by any information available in the files of the Federal Bureau of Investigation, Naval Intelligence, Military Intelligence, and from any other source. On the basis of knowledge gained from all of these sources the actual segregation process got under way late in July of 1943 at which time the WRA center at Tule Lake was designated as the segregation center. The major movement was completed during September and October of 1943 and the bulk of the Manzanar group was moved during the third week of February, 1944. There will be approximately 1500 or 2000 people to be moved to Tule Lake during the next two or three months. This whole process has been complex, time consuming, and it is one of those jobs that may never be completely finished, since new developments may necessitate further denials of leave clearance.

4. The formulation and execution of policies which provide for services to evacuees in relation to their property problems, both personal and real property located within the evacuated area.

This problem has received little public attention but is nevertheless important. The Federal Reserve Bank and the Farm Security Administration in the beginning handled services to evacuees in connection with their property. The Federal Reserve Bank rendered service in the warehousing of personal property and aided in problems connected with urban property, while the Farm Security Administration handled problems connected with rural property. WRA took over the responsibility for these services in August, 1942. A property office was established in San Francisco and sub-offices have been set up in Los Angeles, Sacramento, Portland, and Seattle. Evacuees either owned or operated approximately $200,000,000 worth of property. Much of this is being looked after by agents selected by the evacuees themselves. However, WRA has made provision for warehousing all personal property left on the Coast for those evacuees who wish to have such service. We also help in the sale and leasing of real property if such service is requested by the evacuees and if they provide power of attorney. The job of transporting household goods from local points to key warehouses and from those warehouses to other parts of the country as evacuees continue to relocate is a tremendous one.

5. Relations with other government agencies.

Our major contacts with other government agencies have been with the War and Justice Departments. Throughout the spring, summer, and fall of 1942 a close liaison with the War Department was necessary because of the movement of about 110,000 people from Army assembly centers to relocation centers. During this period Army engineers were responsible for the construction of the ten centers. An agreement has been in effect throughout the existence of the Authority whereby the War Department is responsible for the external guard at relocation centers and for having troops available should a show of force be needed within a center. The Army Quartermaster Corps has done most of the procurement of food, other than that which is produced on the projects themselves, and has also provided procurement service for medical equipment and supplies. Many other matters involve liaison with the Army, including continuous contact with the Western Defense Command relating to evacuee travel in and out of centers located within the evacuated area.

We have had continuous relationships with the Alien Enemy Control Unit, the Immigration and Naturalization Service, and the Federal Bureau of Investigation in the Department of Justice. We have maintained liaison with the State Department in relation to the international aspect of the program, particularly the problem involving exchange of nationals with Japan, and contacts with the Spanish Consul who represents the protecting power for the Japanese government. Other contacts with government agencies involve relationship with the Office of War Information, Treasury Department, particularly the Alien Property Custodian, War Manpower Commission, Federal Security Agency, Civil Service Commission, National Youth Administration, Office of Education, Navy Department, Coast Guard, and others.

Policies controlled by some of these agencies have had a very important effect upon the program of the War Relocation Authority. The War Department, for example, has controlled the policy relating to the evacuated area, including movement of people in and out of that area, and the policy regarding Selective Service as it relates to Japanese Americans. These two matters are of tremendous importance to our program and have required continuous contact throughout. Many policies established by the War Department and other agencies have had a direct or indirect effect upon the morale of both the staff and the evacuees. We have made announcements of procedures that have been agreed upon and then have seen them changed from time to time by certain agencies following the attacks of the Dies Committee or for some other reason. This has had a serious effect on our relationships with evacuees as well as the public at large. While many of these actions did not directly affect a large number of evacuees, they serve to prove to a great majority of them that the government intended to continue to discriminate against American citizens of Japanese ancestry. Specific examples are the revision by the War Department of Selective Service procedures in March, 1942, whereby Japanese Americans were reclassified into 4-F and later into 4-C, which procedures were not changed so as to permit their induction under Selective Service until January, 1944; a change in rules by the Civil Service Commission, after we had worked out definite procedures for examinations and entrance into government service, which set the evacuees apart from other American citizens; initiation of procedures which interfered with merchant ship service by sailors of Japanese ancestry on the East Coast, after we thought we had worked out provisions with the Coast Guard and intelligence agencies; and a reversal of policy by NYA, after we had entered into a training agreement which was running smoothly. This reversal came as a result of the Dies Committee campaign in May and June of 1943.

6. The general problem of public relations.

The problem of acceptance by communities outside the West Coast area of evacuees interested in relocating has been a much simpler one than we had anticipated in the early part of the program. Generally speaking our public relations throughout the Midwest, South and East have been excellent. This is probably due to the fact that we concentrated on these areas, established offices, and developed a staff whose chief job was to secure understanding and acceptance by the public. After the evacuees were moved from the West Coast we assumed our major public relations problem would be in other portions of the country and did not make the provision on the West Coast that we perhaps should have in view of the campaign which has been carried on by the Hearst press, the Native Sons of the Golden West, the California Department of the American Legion, and certain labor groups along the Coast, particularly Dave Beck of the Teamsters Union. This campaign started almost immediately after WRA was established, with demands that the whole program be turned over to the War Department, that all people of Japanese ancestry be excluded from the West Coast for the duration and from the country after the war, that they be interned for the duration and not allowed to relocate in other parts of the country.

These organizations instigated an investigation by the Senate Military Affairs Committee under the leadership of Senator Chandler of Kentucky which began in January, 1943, and continued intermittently throughout the spring, summer, and fall. The results of that investigation did not satisfy certain West Coast interests; consequently, the Dies Committee was brought into the picture in early May, 1943, and has continued since then. Their most intensive drive was made during May, June, and July of 1943 but the investigation continued following the Tule Lake incident in November and I am sure they plan to continue to harass the Authority whenever an opportunity is presented. Our relationship with the West Coast Congressional Delegation has been very good for the most part when considered on an individual basis. A few individuals are quite antagonistic to our program and have carried the torch for the West Coast organizations mentioned above. The outstanding ones in this group are John Costello, Clair Engle, John Phillips, Norris Poulson, Alfred Elliott, and more recently Harry Sheppard. Senator Wallgren was quite antagonistic during 1942, but in recent months has been very quiet and reasonably friendly. Other members of Congress who have supplemented the campaign of West Coast critics are Congressman Rankin of Mississippi, Senator Stewart of Tennessee, and upon occasion Senator Chandler of Kentucky, Senator Reynolds of North Carolina, and Congressman J. Parnell Thomas of New Jersey, a member of the Dies Committee. I may have overlooked a few, but outside of this small group our general relationship with the Congress has been excellent.

We have had the support throughout the United States of hundreds of people of good will who have rendered real service in the relocation aspect of our program in particular, and in doing so have been very helpful in handling the public relations problems. The outstanding organizations that have supported the program are: Federal Council of Churches, Home Missions Council of North America, American Friends Service Comittee, Committee on American Principles and Fair Play (which operates in California, Washington, and Oregon), the YMCA, YWCA, Japanese American Student Relocation Council, Committee on Resettlement of Japanese Americans, Protestant Church Committee for Japanese Service, Common Council for American Unity, Denver Council of Churches, Citizens Committee for Resettlement for Work with Japanese Evacuees, Japanese American Citizens League, American Civil Liberties Union, and others.

Among the members of Congress who have been friendly and helpful are Congressman Eberharter of Pennsylvania, a member of the Dies Committee, Congressman Judd of Minnesota, Senator Murdock and Senator Thomas of Utah, Senator O'Mahoney of Wyoming, Senator Hayden of Arizona, Congressman Chenowith of Colorado, Congressmen Outland, Holifield, Tolan, Will Rogers, Ford, Voorhis, all of California, Congressman Coffee of Washington, and many others who have been sympathetic but not particularly active.

SUMMARY OF PRESENT STATUS AND PROBLEMS AHEAD

At the present time we have nine relocation centers and one segregation center. The Jerome Relocation Center, Denson, Arkansas, will be closed in June, leaving eight relocation centers at the beginning of the next fiscal year. Approximately 92,000 people live in relocation centers and the segregation center. When segregation is completed there will be between 18,000 and 19,000 people at Tule Lake and approximately 70,000 in the other eight or nine centers. Over 18,000 are out on indefinite leave at the present time and about 2,000 on seasonal leave. Our major problems at the present time are the completion of leave clearance hearings and the segregation process, realigning and expediting our relocation program in order to secure family relocation, and public relations -- a problem which is continually stirred up by the organizations mentioned in 6.

As relocation proceeds the character of the population within the centers changes and will continue to do so, leaving a residue of older Issei and young children as compared with the mixed population we had in the beginning. This creates a real problem affecting the relocation program and the administration of the centers. It becomes harder to maintain the American institutions and avoid further Japanization of youngsters. This is a natural development resulting from the draining off of the American citizens in the age group from 18 to 35 or 40, who are most easily relocated. It will become more and more difficult to get families made up largely of very young and older people to relocate in normal communities for several reasons. There will be a smaller number of able-bodied workers, the older people will have some language difficulties, the housing problem is more acute, and they are not sure they can find security in outside communities. We anticipate a continued campaign by West Coast organizations which have funds and personnel to devote to a campaign for the exclusion of people of Japanese ancestry from the West Coast or at least for the prevention of their return during the war.

As the war proceeds and it becomes less essential from a military standpoint to maintain the evacuated area, we have the problem of working out a plan with the Army for an orderly reopening of the evacuated area step by step which will facilitate relocation, avoid violence, and at the same time get the job reasonably well done before the war is finally over, so that evacuees will not have to reestablish themselves during a period when there will be competition with a large number returning from the war.

Property problems on the Coast will continue to exist and will become more troublesome. As time goes on we will need to consider conducting our program in such a way as to have needed information in case post-war claims are presented, and at the same time render adequate service to evacuees who cannot return to the Coast in the meantime. There is, of course, the whole question of post-war relocation in case we don't get the job done during the war period, and that problem has not yet been seriously considered.

Sincerely,
/s/ D. S. Myer
Director

cc: Mr. Fortas
DSMyer:ih
2/29/44

HIRABAYASHI v. UNITED STATES
320 U.S. 81
1943

This was the first of the cases testing the constitutionality of the Presidential evacuation order and the Act of Congress designed to effectuate
that order. The facts of the case are set forth
in the opinion. The second case, Korematsu v.
U.S., 323 U.S. 214, in general followed this
precedent; there were two dissenting opinions,
from Justices Murphy and Jackson. A third
case, Ex parte Endo, 323 U.A. 283, granted a
writ of habeas corpus to a loyal Japanese American, discharging her from custody.

Source: By permission from Documents of American History, Vol. II, 8th
Edition, edited by Henry Steele Commager, New York: Appleton-Century-
Crofts, Educational Division, Meredith Corp., 1968.

On Certificate from the United States Circuit Court of Appeals for the Ninth
Circuit.

STONE, J. Appellant, an American citizen of Japanese ancestry, was convicted in the district court of violating the Act of Congress of March 21,
1942, . . . which makes it a misdemeanor knowingly to disregard restrictions made applicable by a military commander to persons in a military
area prescribed by him as such, all as authorized by an Executive Order
of the President.
    The questions for our decision are whether the particular restriction
violated, namely that all persons of Japanese ancestry residing in such an
area be within their place of residence daily between the hours of 8:00 P.M.
and 6:00 A.M., was adopted by the military commander in the exercise of
an unconstitutional delegation by Congress of its legislative power, and
whether the restriction unconstitutionally discriminated between citizens
of Japanese ancestry and those of other ancestries in violation of the Fifth
Amendment. . . .
    . . . Appellant asserted that the indictment should be dismissed because
he was an American citizen who had never been a subject of and had never
borne allegiance to the Empire of Japan, and also because the Act of March
21, 1942, was an unconstitutional delegation of Congressional power. . . .
    The evidence showed that appellant had failed to report to the Civil Con-
trol Station on May 11 or May 12, 1942, as directed, to register for evacuation from the military area. He admitted failure to do so, and stated it had

at all times been his belief that he would be waiving his rights as an American citizen by so doing. The evidence also showed that for like reason he was away from his place of residence after 8:00 P.M. on May 9, 1942. The jury returned a verdict of guilty on both counts and appellant was sentenced to imprisonment for a term of three months on each, the sentences to run concurrently. . . .

The curfew order which appellant violated, and to which the sanction prescribed by the Act of Congress has been deemed to attach, purported to be issued pursuant to an Executive Order of the President. In passing upon the authority of the military commander to make and execute the order, it becomes necessary to consider in some detail the official action which preceded or accompanied the order and from which it derives its purported authority. . . .

. . . On February 19, 1942, the President promulgated Executive Order No. 9066. The Order recited that "the successful prosecution of the war requires every possible protection against espionage and against sabotage to national-defense material, national-defense premises, and national-defense utilities. . . ."

. . . On March 2, 1942, General DeWitt promulgated Public Proclamation No. 1. The proclamation recited that the entire Pacific Coast "by its geographical location is particularly subject to attack, to attempted invasion by the armed forces of nations with which the United States is now at war, and in connection therewith, is subject to espionage and acts of sabotage, thereby requiring the adoption of military measures necessary to establish safeguards against such enemy operations" . . . .

On March 24, 1942, General DeWitt issued Public Proclamation No. 3. After referring to the previous designation of military areas by Public Proclamations No. 1 and 2, it recited that ". . . the present situation within these Military Areas and Zones requires as a matter of military necessity the establishment of certain regulations pertaining to all enemy aliens and all persons of Japanese ancestry within said Military Areas and Zones . . ." It accordingly declared and established that from and after March 27, 1942, "all alien Japanese, all alien Germans, all alien Italians, and all persons of Japanese ancestry residing or being within the geographical limits of Military Area No. 1 . . . shall be within their place of residence between the hours of 8:00 P.M. and 6:00 A.M., which period is hereinafter referred to as the hours of curfew." It also imposed certain other restrictions on persons of Japanese ancestry, and provided that any person violating the regulations would be subject to the criminal penalties provided by the Act of Congress of March 21, 1942. . . .

Appellant does not deny that he knowingly failed to obey the curfew order as charged in the second count of the indictment, or that the order was authorized by the terms of Executive Order No. 9066, or that the challenged Act of Congress purports to punish with criminal penalties disobedience of such an order. His contentions are only that Congress unconstitutionally delegated its legislative power to the military commander by authorizing him to impose the challenged regulation, and that, even if the regulation were in other respects lawfully authorized, the Fifth Amendment prohibits the discrimination made between citizens of Japanese descent and those of other ancestry.

It will be evident from the legislative history that the Act of March 21, 1942, contemplated and authorized the curfew order which we have before us. . . .

The conclusion is inescapable that Congress, by the Act of March 21, 1942, ratified and confirmed Executive Order No. 9066. . . .

. . . And so far as it lawfully could, Congress authorized and implemented such curfew orders as the commanding officer should promulgate pursuant to the Executive Order of the President. The question then is not one of Congressional power to delegate to the President the promulgation of the Executive Order, but whether, acting in cooperation, Congress and the Executive have constitutional authority to impose the curfew restriction here complained of. . . .

The war power of the national government is "the power to wage war successfully." See Charles Evans Hughes, War Powers Under the Constitution, 42 A.B.A. Rep. 232, 238. It extends to every matter and activity so related to war as substantially to affect its conduct and progress. The power is not restricted to the winning of victories in the field and the repulse of enemy forces. It embraces every phase of the national defense, including the protection of war materials and the members of the armed forces from injury and from the dangers which attend the rise, prosecution and progress of war. . . . Since the Constitution commits to the Executive and to Congress the exercise of the war power in all the vicissitudes and conditions of warfare, it has necessarily given them wide scope for the exercise of judgment and discretion in determining the nature and extent of the threatened injury or danger and in the selection of the means for resisting it. . . . Where, as they did here, the conditions call for the exercise of judgment and discretion and for the choice of means by those branches of the Government on which the Constitution has placed the responsibility of war-making, it is not for any court to sit in review of the wisdom of their action or substitute its judgment for theirs.

The actions taken must be appraised in the light of the conditions with which the President and Congress were confronted in the early months of 1942, many of which, since disclosed, were then peculiarly within the knowledge of the military authorities. . . .

. . . That reasonably prudent men charged with the responsibility of our national defense had ample ground for concluding that they must face the danger of invasion, take measures against it, and in making the choice of measures consider our internal situation, cannot be doubted.

The challenged orders were defense measures for the avowed purpose of safe-guarding the military area in question, at a time of threatened air raids and invasion by the Japanese forces, from the danger of sabotage and espionage. As the curfew was made applicable to citizens residing in the area only if they were of Japanese ancestry, our inquiry must be whether in the light of all the facts and circumstances there was any substantial basis for the conclusion, in which Congress and the military commander united, that the curfew as applied was a protective measure necessary to meet the threat of sabotage and espionage which would substantially affect the war effort and which might reasonably be expected to aid a threatened enemy invasion. The alternative which appellant insists must be accepted is for the military authorities to impose the curfew on all citizens within the military area, or on none. In a case of threatened danger requiring prompt action, it is a choice between inflicting obviously needless hardship on the many, or sitting passive and unresisting in the presence of the threat. We think that constitutional government, in time of war, is not so powerless and does not compel so hard a choice if those charged with the responsibility of our national defense have reasonable ground for believing that the threat is real. . . .

In the critical days of March, 1942, the danger to our war production by sabotage and espionage in this area seems obvious. . . . At a time of threatened Japanese attack upon this country, the nature of our inhabitants' attachments to the Japanese enemy was consequently a matter of grave concern. Of the 126,000 persons of Japanese descent in the United States, citizens and non-citizens, approximately 112,000 resided in California, Oregon and Washington at the time of the adoption of the military regulations. Of these approximately two-thirds are citizens because born in the United States. Not only did the great majority of such persons reside within the Pacific Coast states but they were concentrated in or near three of the large cities, Seattle, Portland and Los Angeles, all in Military Area No. 1.

There is support for the view that social, economic and political conditions which have prevailed since the close of the last century, when the Japanese began to come to this country in substantial numbers, have intensified their solidarity and have in large measure prevented their assimilation as an integral part of the white population. In addition, large numbers of children of Japanese parentage are sent to Japanese language schools outside the regular hours of public schools in the locality. Some of these schools are generally believed to be sources of Japanese nationalistic propaganda, cultivating allegiance to Japan. Considerable numbers, estimated to be approximately 10,000, of American-born children of Japanese parentage have been sent to Japan for all or a part of their education.

Congress and the Executive, including the military commander, could have attributed special significance, in its bearing on the loyalties of persons of Japanese descent, to the maintenance by Japan of its system of dual citizenship. Children born in the United States of Japanese alien parents, and especially those children born before December 1, 1924, are under many circumstances deemed, by Japanese law, to be citizens of Japan. No official census of those whom Japan regards as having thus retained Japanese citizenship is available, but there is ground for the belief that the number is large. . . .

As a result of all these conditions affecting the life of the Japanese, both aliens and citizens, in the Pacific Coast area, there has been relatively little social intercourse between them and the white population. The restrictions, both practical and legal, affecting the privileges and opportunities afforded to persons of Japanese extraction residing in the United States, have been sources of irritation and may well have tended to increase their isolation, and in many instances their attachments to Japan and its institutions.

Viewing these data in all their aspects, Congress and the Executive could reasonably have concluded that these conditions have encouraged the continued attachment of members of this group to Japan and Japanese institutions. These are only some of the many considerations which those charged with the responsibility for the national defense could take into account in determining the nature and extent of the danger of espionage and sabotage, in the event of invasion or air raid attack. The extent of that danger could be definitely known only after the event and after it was too late to meet it. Whatever views we may entertain regarding the loyalty to this country of the citizens of Japanese ancestry, we cannot reject as unfounded the judgment of the military authorities and of Congress that there were disloyal members of that population, whose number and strength could not be precisely and quickly ascertained. We cannot say that the war-making branches of the Government did not have ground for believing that in a critical hour such persons could not readily be isolated and separately dealt with, and constituted a menace to the national defense and safety, which demanded that prompt and adequate measures be taken to guard against it.

Appellant does not deny that, given the danger, a curfew was an appropriate measure against sabotage. It is an obvious protection against the perpetration of sabotage most readily committed during the hours of darkness. If it was an appropriate exercise of the war power its validity is not impaired because it has restricted the citizen's liberty. Like every military control of the population of a dangerous zone in war time, it necessarily involves some infringment of individual liberty, just as does the police establishment of fire lines during a fire, or the confinement of people to their houses during an air raid alarm -- neither of which could be thought to be an infringement of constitutional right. Like them, the validity of the restraints of the curfew order depends on all the conditions which obtain at the time the curfew is imposed and which support the order imposing it.

But appellant insists that the exercise of the power is inappropriate and unconstitutional because it discriminates against citizens of Japanese ancestry, in violation of the Fifth Amendment. The Fifth Amendment contains no equal protection clause and it restrains only such discriminatory legislation by Congress as amounts to a denial of due process. Congress may hit at a particular danger where it is seen, without providing for others which are not so evident or so urgent.

Distinctions between citizens solely because of their ancestry are by their very nature odious to a free people whose institutions are founded upon the doctrine of equality. For that reason, legislative classification or discrimination based on race alone has often been held to be a denial of equal protection. We may assume that these considerations would be controlling here were it not for the fact that the danger of espionage and sabotage, in time of war and of threatened invasion, calls upon the military authorities to scrutinize every relevant fact bearing on the loyalty of populations in the danger areas. Because racial discriminations are in most circumstances irrelevant and therefore prohibited, it by no means follows that, in dealing with the perils of war, Congress and the Executive are wholly precluded from taking into account those facts and circumstances which are relevant to measures for our national defense and for the successful prosecution of the war, and which may in fact place citizens of one ancestry in a different category from others. "We must never forget, that it is a constitution we are expounding," "a constitution intended to endure for ages to come, and, consequently, to be adapted to the various crises of human affairs." The adoption by Government, in the crisis of war and of threatened invasion, of measures for the public safety, based upon the recognition of facts and circumstances which indicate that a group of one national extraction may menace that safety more than others, is not wholly beyond the limits of the Constitution and is not to be condemned merely because in other and in most circumstances racial distinctions are irrelevant.

Here the aim of Congress and the Executive was the protection against sabotage of war materials and utilities in areas thought to be in danger of Japanese invasion and air attack. We have stated in detail facts and circumstances with respect to the American citizens of Japanese ancestry residing on the Pacific Coast which support the judgment of the war-waging branches of the Government that some restrictive measure was urgent. We cannot say that these facts and circumstances, considered in the particular war setting, could afford no ground for differentiating citizens of Japanese ancestry from other groups in the United States. The fact alone that attack on our shores was threatened by Japan rather than another enemy power set these citizens apart from others who have no particular associations with Japan. . . .

The Constitution as a continuously operating charter of government does not demand the impossible or the impractical. The essentials of the legislative function are preserved when Congress authorizes a statutory command to become operative, upon ascertainment of a basic conclusion of fact by a designated representative of the Government. The present statute, which authorized curfew orders to be made pursuant to Executive Order No. 9066 for the protection of war resources from espionage and sabotage, satisfies those requirements. Under the Executive Order the basic facts, determined by the military commander in the light of knowledge then available, were whether that danger existed and whether a curfew order was an appropriate means of minimizing the danger. Since his findings to that effect were, as we have said, not without adequate support, the legislative function was performed and the sanction of the statute attached to violations of the curfew

order. It is unnecessary to consider whether or to what extent such findings would support orders differing from the curfew order.

The conviction under the second count is without constitutional infirm-
ity. Hence we have no occasion to review the conviction on the first count
since, as already stated, the sentences on the two counts are to run concurrently and conviction on the second is sufficient to sustain the sentence.
For this reason also it is unnecessary to consider the Government's argument that compliance with the order to report at the Civilian Control Station
did not necessarily entail confinement in a relocation center.

Affirmed.

MEMORANDUM FORWARDED TO DILLON S. MYER BY ASSISTANT
SECRETARY McCLOY - June 15, 1944

Source: Uprooted Americans: Japanese Americans and the War Relocation
Authority During World War II, Dillon S. Myer, Tucson: University of
Arizona Press, copyright 1971.

Subject: Nisei.

1. A report by Lt. Colonel Marcel G. Crombez, AGF Special Representative in CBI, * contains the following which will be of interest to you in
connection with Nisei training.

a. The Nisei personnel which were attached to First Galahad (475th
Infantry Regiment) have proven to be of great value to that organization.
In every instance the men have been loyal and demonstrated great courage
in carrying out their assignments.

b. They have proven their usefulness in the following manner:

(1) Interpreting for U.S. officers Japanese commands which were
     clearly distinguishable in close combat in which this organization
     took part.

(2) Translating, identifying, and selecting important Japanese docu-
     ments for immediate dispatch to higher headquarters.

(3) As interpreters accompanying patrols.

c. One incident is worthy of note. During the early stages of the campaign in the Mogaung Valley the Second Galahad Battalion, executing a flank-
ing movement, was surrounded by Jap elements for a period of thirteen
days. During the last day the Japanese attacked the Second Battalion's position sixteen times. Each time the battalion commander was able to anticipate the direction of the attack due to the fact that the Nisei attached to
his staff were able to overhear the Jap officers' instructions which they
were shouting to their subordinates. The visibility in the area averaged
20 to 30 yards, and the attacking force was but 20 to 70 yards away, and
the commands could be clearly heard. Through the interpretation of their
commands the Second Battalion Commander, Lt. Colonel George A. Magee,
Jr. was able to shift his troops to block the main Jap effort and to concen-
trate his fire on the Japs as they endeavored to penetrate the battalion's
lines. At the end of the day the interpreters told the battalion commander
that the Jap officers were reprimanding the Jap soldiers for lack of courage,

---

*The China-Burma-India theater.

to which the soldiers were replying and offering as an excuse the numbers that had been killed or were missing.

/s/ W. H. Wood
Colonel, G.S.C.
Chief, Asiatic Theatre
Theatre Group, OPD

AMENDMENT TO THE NATIONAL ACT OF 1940,
PUBLIC LAW NO. 405, 78th CONGRESS
July 1, 1944

(i) Making in the United States a formal written renunciation of nationality in such form as may be prescribed
by and before such officer as may be designated by,
the Attorney General, whenever the United States shall
be in a state of war and the Attorney General shall approve such renunciation as not contrary to the interests
of national defense.

Signed by the President on July 1, 1944
as Public Law 405 (78th Congress)

CONFIDENTIAL LETTER FROM WRA DIRECTOR MYER
TO ALL PROJECT DIRECTORS
December 8, 1944

Source: By permission from Uprooted Americans: Japanese Americans and
the War Relocation Authority During World War II, Dillon S. Myer, Tucson:
University of Arizona Press, copyright 1971.

DEPARTMENT OF THE INTERIOR
WAR RELOCATION AUTHORITY
Washington

CONFIDENTIAL

TO: All Project Directors

Attached is a copy of a general statement covering certain policy decisions that have now been made in connection with the lifting of the West
Coast exclusion orders. A supply of additional copies is being forwarded
to you for general distribution both to the staff and to the evacuees. This
material, however, should be held in strict confidence until you get word
from this office.

You will note that we have scheduled the closing of all relocation centers within one year. Our job now is to see that this is done and that all of
the eligible people now residing in the centers are located either in the former evacuated zone or elsewhere in the United States. I cannot impress
too strongly on you that this is our job and that we must accomplish it.

It is tremendously important to everyone concerned that the final program of liquidating the relocation centers be completed while there is a
good demand for workers throughout the country in war plants, in civilian
goods production, service occupations and in food production. As we ap-
proach the end of the war, these opportunities will not be so plentiful and
if liquidation of the program should be postponed until that time, our task
would be immeasurably harder. It will be almost impossible if evacuees
have to compete with returning soldiers and with other people who may be
seeking adjustment during the reconversion project.

The announcement of the reopening of the Coast area will be received
by many of the evacuees as welcome news. The closing of the relocation
centers, however, will be interpreted by some as the loss of sanctuary
and security. You should see that all of the evacuees understand the basic
policies of the War Relocation Authority with regard to the closing of the
centers. All questions should be answered firmly and positively but in a
courteous manner and without the use of threats of any kind. Much will de-
pend on the diplomacy and sound judgment which you and members of your
staff show in this regard.

In discussing relocation to the West Coast with evacuees, Project Directors and their staffs should proceed at all times on the basic assumption that the movement will be an orderly one and that returning evacuees will be readily accepted by their friends and neighbors. Any tendency to discuss possible dangers or potentialities of violence should be discouraged.

There will be questions as to why the centers are to be closed before the end of the war. The answer is obvious, that with the lifting of the restrictions on the Coast, the great majority of the people of Japanese ancestry are now free to go anywhere and the reason for which the relocation centers were established no longer exists. They are being kept in operation during the final period of the program so that center residents will have ample time and opportunity for the development of sound relocation plans. The opportunity for resettlement now is far better than it would be at the end of the war. Resettlement now is for the benefit of the evacuees.

Some will ask what the War Relocation Authority will do if certain individuals or groups do not relocate.

The answer should be simply that we don't think anyone will actually refuse. Ample provision is being made so that each individual may make a satisfactory transition back to private life.

There will be some who will want to know whether the War Relocation Authority will make loans for farm or business financing. The answer should be that the War Relocation Authority is not a lending agency and has no intention of becoming one. There are other Federal agencies equipped with authority and funds to take care of such needs.

There will be evacuees who will want to regain possession of their land or other property in the Coast area immediately. Some may wish to break leases or institute legal proceedings for the ejection of tenants. Such action should be discouraged wherever possible, because it will certainly result in adverse publicity and make the job of orderly resettlement more difficult, not only for the individual concerned but for other evacuees.

You will, of course, realize that there are some detailed points of policy which have been determined but which have not been covered in the general statement for distribution to the evacuees. We are supplying some of this information to you below, and we will furnish more as additional policy decisions are made, so that you can make it available to key members of your staff.

There may be citizen evacuees who will want to know whether renunciation of citizenship under the recent law passed by Congress will mean that they would remain in or be sent to Tule Lake until the end of hostilities with Japan. The War Relocation Authority will not make any further determinations under leave clearance procedures. The Army authorities now designate those [whose movements will be restrained or] who will not be eligible to return to the West Coast area. Doubtless a renunciation of citizenship, if accepted by the Attorney General of the United States, would result in some action by the military -- possibly a recommendation for internment, but it is not the responsibility of the War Relocation Authority.

The lifting of the West Coast ban means that any individual (except those who may be designated by the War Department for further investigation) may leave the relocation center at any time. Assistance, however, will be given only to those who have an approved plan of relocation. We believe it is desirable to give this assistance and to supervise the movement of the people for their own interest but there is no reason why an eligible individual or family may not leave of his own choice without regard to any plan or assistance which the War Relocation Authority may offer. Likewise, they are free to remain residents of the relocation centers while the centers are operated, provided they conduct themselves in such a manner as not to disrupt the center operations or interfere with the relocation program. We have no obligation to provide center residence for those who are now free to return to their former homes unless they are willing to abide by project regulations and help in maintaining a peaceful community.

There may be questions about purchase of Government property now in use at the projects. This will all be sold through regular surplus property procedure as indicated in our policy statement.

You may have individuals who will want to make brief trips to the evacuated area for the purpose of scouting or for the disposal of property. It may be distinctly understood that any such travel will be at the evacuee's own expense and that he must secure short term leave for this purpose. Otherwise he will not be readmitted to the center. Reinductions to the center should be kept to a minimum, involving students at the end of the school year or others who are entitled to such readmission. Likewise, visits to centers should be permitted only where the visiting evacuee has secured the approval of the appropriate relocation office or (in the case of visiting between centers) of the Project Director at the center where the visiting evacuee resides.

Unless this policy is rigidly enforced and strongly impressed on the minds of the evacuees, there may be a widespread tendency for relocated evacuees to leave their jobs without proper War Manpower Commission clearance, and there may also be serious transportation congestion in the vicinity of the centers. Consequently we are authorizing you as Project Director to deny admission to all evacuees who attempt to visit your center without securing proper clearance in advance.

Applications for repatriation or expatriation are no longer factors to be considered in relocation planning. Also the WRA "stop list" will no longer be taken into consideration in connection with departures from the relocation centers. The Army now has full responsibility for designating those persons whose freedom of movement is to be restrained. A new stop list will be provided by the War Department. There will be family members in the centers where the breadwinner is in internment and this will be given as a reason why the family cannot successfully relocate. These people should be encouraged to make application to live in a family internment camp, or to relocate despite the absence of the breadwinner. We should at all times recognize, as we have in the past, the right of the older and

more mature children to make their own decisions, in situations involving
family residence in an internment camp or the right to resume normal
lives in American communities.

/s/ D. S. Myer
Director

cc: Mr. Cozzens
Director's copy
AMarkley:mh
12/7/44

EDITORIAL FROM THE WASHINGTON POST BY ALAN BARTH
March 28, 1946

Job Well Done

The most distasteful of all war jobs, the detention upon mere suspicion and without trial of approximately 120,000 persons of Japanese ancestry, two-thirds of them citizens of the United States, has now been liquidated. It was a job made necessary through the decision early in 1942 of Gen. John L. DeWitt to exclude all Japanese-Americans from the Western Defense Command, of which he was at that time the commander. His exclusion order has since been validated by the Supreme Court on grounds of military necessity. For our part, however, we hold still to the opinion we have expressed on a number of occasions that the exclusion was altogether unnecessary, that it was prompted much more by blind racial prejudice than by military considerations and that the Supreme Court's validation of it amounted, as Mr. Justice Murphy charged in a dissenting opinion, to a "legalization of racism." The treatment accorded this helpless minority remains a smudge upon our national honor and a threat to elementary principles of freedom.

Once the exclusion error was committed, guardianship of the uprooted Japanese-Americans became a Federal responsibility. They had to be kept in detention centers until they could be relocated in parts of the country other than the West Coast. The burden of discharging this unhappy obligation was given to an emergency agency, the War Relocation Authority, headed at first by Milton Eisenhower, later and through most of its existence by Dillon S. Myer. It performed its task with humanity, with efficiency and with a conscientious sense of trusteeship toward the evacuees which made some amends for the terrible hardship inflicted upon them. All the men associated in this undertaking, and in particular Mr. Myer, who fought valiantly and pertinaciously against prejudice for the rights of these unfortunates in his charge, can take pride in a difficult job exceedingly well done.

When at last the Army rescinded its exclusion order about 57,500 evacuees moved back to their former homes in the West Coast States. But about 51,800 settled eastward in new homes. Perhaps the dispersal will have some benefits in better integration of the Japanese-Americans into the American society. The loyalty of those left here has been meticulously scrutinized. Out of the whole number in the relocation centers, some 3000, including quite innocent family members, were transferred to internment camps administered by the Department of Justice; and about 4700 persons were voluntarily repatriated to Japan -- many of them, no doubt, because the treatment they received here convinced them they had no hope of leading free lives in America. It seems to us that we owe those who remain generous help in getting reestablished and restitution for their property losses.

CITATION PRESENTED TO DILLON S. MYER,
BY THE JAPANESE AMERICAN CITIZENS LEAGUE
May 22, 1946

TO DILLON S. MYER

American and champion of human rights and common decency
Whose courageous and inspired leadership as
National Director of the War Relocation Authority
Against war hysteria, race prejudice, and misguided hate, as
     well as economic greed draped in patriotic colors,
Contributed mightily in convincing the American Government
     and public at large
That Americans of Japanese ancestry and their resident alien
     parents
Were, and are, loyal and sincere Americans worthy of every
     right and privilege of the American heritage,
And aided materially in restoring faith and conviction in the
     American way
To these same Americans of Japanese ancestry and their resident
     alien parents
Who were evacuated without trial or hearing by military fiat
     from their homes and associations on the West Coast in the
     spring of 1942,
Relocated in government centers in the wastelands of the west,
And then resettled throughout the United States as proven Americans.

TO DILLON S. MYER

Who so capably and ably administered the War Relocation Authority under
the most difficult of circumstances and against the most vicious of opposition in a manner which commended him to the American people and the
evacuee population at large, this testimonial scroll is gratefully presented
by the Japanese-American Citizens League and their friends at this banquet
in his honor at the Roosevelt Hotel, New York City, May 22, 1946.

COLUMN BY HAROLD L. ICKES, IN THE WASHINGTON EVENING STAR
September 23, 1946

Harold L. Ickes
MAN TO MAN

WARTIME ABUSE OF AMERICAN JAPANESE
SHOULD NOW BE CORRECTED BY U.S.

I hope that those who are disposed to be indifferent about our treatment
of alien strains will read "Citizen 13660", written by Mine Okubo and published by the Columbia University Press. Both the illustrations and the
short text tell, without the rancor that would be understandable, of the
treatment of the Japanese who were living in this "land of the brave and
home of the free" at the time of the attack on Pearl Harbor.

As a member of President Roosevelt's administration, I saw the United
States Army give way to mass hysteria over the Japanese. The investigation of Pearl Harbor disclosed that the Army in Hawaii was more intent upon acts of anticipated sabotage that never occurred than in being alert
against a possible surprise attack by the Japanese.

On the mainland, the Army had taken no precautionary measures.
Then suddenly it lost its self-control and, egged on by public clamor, some
of it from greedy Americans who sought an opportunity to possess themselves of Japanese rights and property, it began to round up indiscriminate-
ly the Japanese who had been born in Japan, as well as those born here.

Crowded into cars like cattle, these hapless people were hurried away
to hastily constructed and thoroughly inadequate concentration camps, with
soldiers with nervous muskets on guard, in the great American desert.
We gave the fancy name of "relocation centers" to these dust bowls, but
they were concentration camps nonetheless, although not as bad as Dachau
or Buchenwald.

Hate Kept at Fever Heat

War-excited imaginations, raw race-prejudice and crass greed kept
hateful public opinion along the Pacific Coast at fever heat. Fortunately,
the President had put at the head of the War Relocation Authority a strong
and able man who was not afraid to fight back. Later the President transferred the agency to the Department of the Interior. I claim no credit for
the result that was finally attained except that I stood shoulder to shoulder
with Dillon Myer and let my own fists fly on occasion. Mr. Myer fully de-
served the Medal for Merit which he was later awarded.

It was to be expected that some native-born Japanese would have to be
watched closely. Some wanted to go back to Japan and help has been given

them. But, generally speaking, the Japanese, particularly those who had been born in this country and were therefore American citizens, have settled back into American communities and there is no reason to believe that they will not continue to be loyal Americans.

If we Americans, with the Army in the lead, made fools of ourselves for which we ought properly to be ashamed, it must be said that the American Japanese, with very few exceptions, gave an example of human dignity by which all of us might profit. However, they have not had returned to them the property that was rifled from them, or its equivalent.

Property Should Be Restored

A bill was introduced in the recent session of Congress setting up a commission to pass upon the claims of these dispossessed American Japanese for property of which they were despoiled. This bill ought to pass and no time should be lost in making restitution for property that was lost or misappropriated.

If the Japanese had been permitted to continue their normal lives they would have occasioned slight concern. They did not in Hawaii where the proportion of Japanese is much larger than in any State on the mainland and where the temptation to favor Japan was necessarily much greater.

No soldiers wearing the American uniform gave a better account of themselves than did the American-born Japanese. Japanese troops, both from Hawaii and the mainland, as the Army records will show, were outstanding for bravery, intelligence, endurance and daring. Their loyalty was not only unimpeachable, but remarkable, considering the affronts and injustices that had been put upon them and their people.

This whole episode was one in which we can take no pride. To understand just what we did to many thousands of our fellow Americans, we should read "Citizen 13660."

TAKAHASHI v. FISH AND GAME COMMISSION
1947

TORAO TAKAHASHI
v.
FISH AND GAME COMMISSION, Lee F. Payne, as Chairman thereof,
and W.B. Williams, Harvey E. Hastain, and William Silva,
as Members thereof
(334 US 410-431.)

Summary

A California statute forbidding the issuance of commercial fishing licenses to aliens ineligible to citizenship was held in an opinion by BLACK,
J., in which six other Justices joined, to violate the constitutional right of
such aliens to the equal protection of the laws. The contention that the statute might be supported as a conservation measure was rejected.

MURPHY, J., in whose opinion RUTLEDGE, J., joined, expressed
agreement with these views, but thought that the statute should also be condemned as being the direct outgrowth of antagonism toward persons of Japanese ancestry and as having no relation whatever to any constitutionally
cognizable interest of California.
REED, J., in whose opinion JACKSON, J., joined, dissented on the
ground that a state has the power to exclude all aliens from enjoyment of
its natural resources, including its fisheries, and that a classification ex-
cluding such aliens as are ineligible to citizenship is not unreasonable.

Mr. Justice Murphy, with whom Mr. Justice Rutledge agrees, concurring.
The opinion of the Court, in which I join, adequately expresses my
views as to all but one important aspect of this case. That aspect relates
to the fact that § 990 of the California Fish and Game Code, barring those
ineligible to citizenship from securing commercial fishing licenses, is the
direct outgrowth of antagonism toward persons of Japanese ancestry. Even
the most cursory examination of the background of the statute demonstrates
that it was designed solely to discriminate against such persons in a manner inconsistent with the concept of equal protection of the laws. Legislation of that type is not entitled to wear the cloak of constitutionality.
The statute in question is but one more manifestation of the anti-Japanese fever which has been evident in California in varying degrees
*[423]
since the turn of the century. *See concurring opinion in Oyama v. California, 332 US 633, 650, ante, 249, 261, 68 S Ct 269, and dissenting opinion
in Korematsu v. United States, 323 US 214, 233, 89 L ed 194, 207, 65 S Ct

193. That fever, of course, is traceable to the refusal or the inability of certain groups to adjust themselves economically and socially relative to residents of Japanese ancestry. For some years prior to the Japanese attack on Pearl Harbor, these protagonists of intolerance had been leveling unfounded accusations and innuendoes against Japanese fishing crews operating off the coast of California. These fishermen numbered about a thousand and most of them had long resided in that state. It was claimed that they were engaged not only in fishing but in espionage and other illicit activities on behalf of the Japanese Government. As war with Japan approached and finally became a reality, these charges were repeated with increasing vigor. Yet full investigations by appropriate authorities failed to reveal any competent supporting evidence; not even one Japanese fisherman was arrested for alleged espionage. Such baseless accusations can only be viewed as an integral part of the long campaign to undermine the reputation of persons of Japanese background and to discourage their residence in California. See McWilliams Prejudice (1944), C VII.

More specifically, these accusations were used to secure the passage of discriminatory fishing legislation. But such legislation was not immediately forthcoming. The continued presence in California of the Japanese fishermen without the occurrence of any untoward incidents on their part served for a time as adequate and living refutation of the propaganda. Then came the evacuation of all persons of Japanese ancestry from the West Coast. See Korematsu v. United States (US) supra. Once evacuation was achieved, an intensive campaign was begun to prevent the return to
*[424]
California of the evacuees. *All of the old charges, including the ones relating to the fishermen, were refurbished and augmented. This time the Japanese were absent and were unable to provide effective opposition. The winds of racial animosity blew unabated.

During the height of this racial storm in 1943, numerous anti-Japanese bills were considered by the California legislators. Several amendments to the Alien Land Law were enacted. And §990 of the Fish and Game Code was altered to provide that "A commercial fishing license may be issued to any person other than an alien Japanese." No pretense was made that this alteration was in the interests of conservation. It was made at a time when all alien Japanese were excluded from California, with no immediate return indicated; thus the banning of fishing licenses for them could have no early effect upon the conservation of fish. Moreover, the period during which this amendment was passed was one in which both federal and state authorities were doing their utmost to encourage greater food production for wartime purposes. The main desire at this time was to increase rather than to decrease the catch of fish. Certainly the contemporaneous bulletins and reports of the Bureau of Marine Fisheries of California did not indicate the existence of any conservation problem due to an excess number of fishermen. See Thirty-Eighth Biennial Report (July 1, 1944), pp 33-36; Fish Bulletin No 58, for the year 1940; Fish Bulletin No 59, for the years 1941 and 1942.

These circumstances only confirm the obvious fact that the 1943 amendment to § 990 was intended to discourage the return to California of Japanese aliens. By taking away their commercial fishing rights, the lives of those aliens who plied the fisherman's trade would be made more difficult and unremunerative. And the non-Japanese fishermen would thereby be free from the com-

*[425]

petition *afforded by these aliens. The equal protection clause of the Fourteenth Amendment, however, does not permit a state to discriminate against resident aliens in such a fashion, whether the purpose be to give effect to racial animosity or to protect the competitive interests of other residents.

The 1945 amendment to § 990 which is now before us stands in no better position than the 1943 amendment. This later alteration eliminated the reference to "alien Japanese" and substituted therefor "a person ineligible to citizenship." Adoption of this change also occurred during a period when anti-Japanese agitation in California had reached one of its periodic peaks. The announcement of the end of the Japanese exclusion orders, plus this Court's decision in Ex parte Endo, 323 US 283, 89 L ed 243, 65 S Ct 208, made the return to California of many of the evacuees a reasonable certainty. The prejudices, the antagonisms and the hatreds were once again aroused, punctuated this time by numerous acts of violence against the returning Japanese Americans. Another wave of anti-Japanese proposals marked the 1945 legislative session. It was in this setting that the amendment to § 990 was proposed and enacted in 1945.

It is of interest and significance that the amendment in question was proposed by a legislative committee devoted to Japanese resettlement problems, not by a committee concerned with the conservation of fish. The Senate Fact-Finding Committee on Japanese Resettlement issued a report on May 1, 1945. This report dealt with such matters as the Alien Land Law, the Japanese language schools, dual citizenship and the Tule Lake riot. And under the heading "Japanese Fishing Boats" (pp 5-6) appeared this explanation of the proposed amendment to § 990:

*[426]

*"The committee gave little consideration to the problems of the use of fishing vessels on our coast owned and operated by Japanese, since this matter seems to have previously been covered by legislation. The committee, however, feels that there is danger of the present statute being declared unconstitutional, on the grounds of discrimination, since it is directed against alien Japanese. It is believed that this legal question can probably be eliminated by an amendment which has been proposed to the bill which would make it apply to any alien who is ineligible to citizenship. The committee has introduced Senate Bill 413 to make this change in the statute."

Not a word was said in this report regarding the need for the conservation of fish or the necessity of limiting the number of fishermen. The obvious thought behind the amendment was to attempt to legalize the discrimination against Japanese alien fishermen by dropping the specific reference to them.

The proposed revision was adopted. The trial court below correctly
described the situation as follows: "As it was commonly known to the legislators of 1945 that Japanese were the only aliens ineligible to citizenship
who engaged in commercial fishing in ocean waters bordering on California,
and as the Court must take judicial notice of the same fact, it becomes mani-
fest that in enacting the present version of Section 990, the Legislature intended thereby to eliminate alien Japanese from those entitled to a commercial fishing license by means of description rather than by name. To all
intents and purposes and in effect the provision in the 1943 and 1945 amendments are the same, the thin veil used to conceal a purpose being too trans-
parent. Under each and both, alien Japanese are denied a right to a license
to catch fish on the high

*[427]

seas for *profit, and to bring them to shore for the purpose of selling the
same in a fresh state . . . this discrimination constitutes an unequal ex-
action and a greater burden upon the persons of the class named than that
imposed upon others in the same calling and under the same conditions, and
amounts to prohibition. This discrimination, patently hostile, is not based
upon a reasonable ground of classification and, to that extent, the section
is in violation of §1 of the Fourteenth Amendment to the Constitution of the
United States, ..."

We should not blink at the fact that § 990, as now written, is a discriminatory piece of legislation having no relation whatever to any constitutionally cognizable interest of California. It was drawn against a background
of racial and economic tension. It is directed in spirit and in effect solely
against aliens of Japanese birth. It denies them commercial fishing rights
not because they threaten the success of any conservation program, not because their fishing activities constitute a clear and present danger to the
welfare of California or of the nation, but only because they are of Japanese
stock, a stock which has had the misfortune to arouse antagonism among
certain powerful interests. We need but unbutton the seemingly innocent
words of §990 to discover beneath them the very negation of all the ideals
of the equal protection clause. No more is necessary to warrant a reversal
of the judgment below.

McCARRAN INTERNAL SECURITY ACT
September 23, 1950

(Public Law 831, 81st Congress)

The growth of Communist power in the postwar world aroused deep
fears among many Americans who believed that Communism menaced
America not only from without but from within. In 1947, President
Truman inaugurated a loyalty program designed to keep the federal
government free from subversive influence. In 1950, Congress went
beyond the Truman program and acted to limit the operation of "subversive" groups in all areas of American life. Ignoring President
Truman's warning that the act was unconstitutional, Congress over-
rode his veto by a voice-vote.

Source: By permission from Documents of American History, Vol. II,
8th Edition, edited by Henry Steele Commager, New York: Appleton-
Century-Crofts, Educational Division, Meredith Corp., 1968.

AN ACT

To protect the United States against certain unAmerican and subversive
activities by requiring registration of Communist organizations, and
for other purposes.

Sec. 2. As a result of evidence adduced before various committees
of the Senate and House of Representatives, the Congress hereby finds
that --

(1) There exists a world Communist movement which, in its
origins, its development, and its present practice, is a world-
wide revolutionary movement whose purpose it is, by treachery,
deceit, infiltration into other groups (governmental and otherwise), espionage, sabotage, terrorism, and any other means
deemed necessary, to establish a Communist totalitarian dictatorship in the countries throughout the world through the me-
dium of world-wide Communist organization. . . .

(4) The direction and control of the world Communist movement is vested in and exercised by the Communist dictatorship
of a foreign country.

(5) The Communist movement in the United States is an organization numbering thousands of adherents, rigidly and ruth-
lessly disciplined. Awaiting and seeking to advance a moment
when the United States may be so far extended by foreign en-
gagements, so far divided in counsel, or so far in industrial or
financial straits, that overthrow of the Government of the United
States by force and violence may seem possible of achievement,
it seeks converts far and wide by an extensive system of school-
ing and indoctrination. Such preparations by Communist organizations in other countries have aided in supplanting existing

governments. The Communist organization in the United States, pursuing its stated objectives, the recent successes of Communist methods in other countries, and the nature and control of the world Communist movement itself, present a clear and present danger to the security of the United States and to the existence of free American institutions, and make it necessary that Congress, in order to provide for the common defense, to preserve the sovereignty of the United States as an independent nation, and to guarantee to each State a republican form of government, enact appropriate legislation recognizing the existence of such world-wide conspiracy and designed to prevent it from accomplishing its purpose in the United States. . . .

Sec. 4. (a) It shall be unlawful for any person knowingly to combine, conspire, or agree with any other person to perform any act which would substantially contribute to the establishment within the United States of a totalitarian dictatorship, as defined in paragraph (15) of section 3 of this title, the direction and control of which is to be vested in, or exercised by or under the domination or control of, any foreign government, foreign organization, or foreign individual: Provided, however, That this subsection shall not apply to the proposal of constitutional amendment. . . .

(f) Neither the holding of office nor membership in any Communist organization by any person shall constitute per se a violation of subsection (a) or subsection (c) of this section or of any other criminal statute. The fact of the registration of any person under section 7 or section 8 of this title as an officer or member of any Communist organization shall not be received in evidence against such person in any prosecution for any alleged violation of subsection (a) or subsection (c) of this section or for any alleged violation of any other criminal statute. . . .

Sec. 7. (a) Each Communist action organization (including any organization required, by a final order of the Board, to register as a Communist-action organization) shall, within the time specified in subsection (c) of this section, register with the Attorney General, or on a form prescribed by him by regulations, as a Communist-action organization.

(b) Each Communist-front organization. . . shall. . . register with the Attorney General, on a form prescribed by him by regulations as a Communist-front organization. . . .

(d) Upon the registration of each Communist organization under the provisions of this title, the Attorney General shall publish in the Federal Register the fact that such organization has registered as a Communist-action organization, or as a Communist-front organization, as the case may be, and the publication thereof shall constitute notice to all members of such organization that such organization has so registered. . . .

Sec. 12. (a) There is hereby established a board, to be known as the Subversive Activities Control Board, which shall be composed of five members, who shall be appointed by the President, by and with the advice and consent of the Senate. Not more than three members of the Board shall be members of the same political party. Two of the original

members shall be appointed for a term of one year, two for a term of
two years, and one for a term of three years, but their successors shall
be appointed for terms of three years each, except that any individual
chosen to fill a vacancy shall be appointed only for the unexpired term
of the member whom he shall succeed. The President shall designate
one member to serve as Chairman of the Board. Any member of the
Board may be removed by the President, upon notice and hearing, for
neglect of duty or malfeasance in office, but for no other cause. . . .

(e) It shall be the duty of the Board --

(1) upon application made by the Attorney General under
section 13 (a) of this title, or by any organization under section 13 (b) of this title, to determine whether any organization
is a "Communist-action organization" within the meaning of
paragraph (3) of section 3 of this title, or a "Communist-front
organization" within the meaning of paragraph (4) of section
3 of this title; and

(2) upon application made by the Attorney General under section 13 (a) of this title, or by any individual under section 13 (b)
of this title, to determine whether any individual is a member
of any Communist-action organization registered, or by final
order of the Board required to be registered under section 7
(a) of this title. . . .

Sec. 22. The Act of October 16, 1918. . . is hereby amended to read
as follows: "That any alien who is a member of any one of the following
classes shall be excluded from admission into the United States:

"(1) Aliens who seek to enter the United States whether solely,
principally, or incidentally, to engage in activities which would
be prejudicial to the public interest, or would endanger the
welfare or safety of the United States;

"(2) Aliens who, at any time, shall be or shall have been members of any of the following classes:

"(A) Aliens who are anarchists;

"(B) Aliens who advocate or teach, or who are members
of or affiliated with any organization that advocates or
teaches, opposition to all organized government;

"(C) Aliens who are members of or affiliated with (i)
the Communist Party of the United States; (ii) any other
totalitarian party of the United States; (iii) the Communist
Political Association; (iv) the Communist or other totalitarian party of any State of the United States, of any foreign state, or of any political or geographical subdivision
of any foreign state; (v) any section, subsidiary, branch,
affiliate, or subdivision of any such association or party;
or (vi) the direct predecessors or successors of any such
association or party, regardless of what name such group
or organization may have used, may now bear, or may hereafter adopt;

"(D) Aliens not within any of the other provisions of this
paragraph (2) who advocate the economic, international,
and governmental doctrines of world communism or the

economic and governmental doctrines of any other form of totalitarianism, or who are members of or affiliated with any organization that advocates the economic, international, and governmental doctrines of world communism, or the economic and governmental doctrines of any other form of totalitarianism, either through its own utterances or through any written or printed publications issued or published by or with the permission or consent of or under the authority of such organization or paid for by the funds of such organizations. . . .

"(F) Aliens who advocate or teach or who are members of or affiliated with any organization that advocates or teaches (i) the overthrow by force or violence or other unconstitutional means of the Government of the United States or of all forms of law; or (ii) the duty, necessity, or propriety of the unlawful assaulting or killing of any officer or officers (either of specific individuals or of officers generally) of the Government of the United States or of any other organized government, because of his or their official character; or (iii) the unlawful damage, injury, or destruction of property; or (iv) sabotage;

"(G) Aliens who write or publish, or cause to be written or published, or who knowingly circulate, distribute, print, or display, or knowingly cause to be circulated, distributed, printed, published, or displayed, or who knowingly have in their possession for the purpose of circulation, publication, or display, any written or printed matter, advocating or teaching opposition to all organized government, or advocating (i) the overthrow by force or violence or other unconstitutional means of the Government of the United States or of all forms of law; or (ii) the duty, necessity, or propriety of the unlawful assaulting or killing of any officer or officers (either of specific individuals or of officers generally) of the Government of the United States or of any other organized government; or (iii) the unlawful damage, injury, or destruction of property; or (iv) sabotage; or (v) the economic, international, and governmental doctrines of world communism or the economic and governmental doctrines of any other form of totalitarianism. . . .

Sec. 102. (a) In the event of any one of the following:

(1) Invasion of the territory of the United States or its possessions,

(2) Declaration of war by Congress, or

(3) Insurrection within the United States in aid of a foreign enemy,

and if, upon the occurrence of one or more of the above, the President shall find that the proclamation of an emergency pursuant to this section is essential to the preservation, protection and defense of the Constitution, and to the common defense and safety of the territory and people of the United States, the President is authorized to make public proclamation of the existence of an "Internal Security Emergency."

(b) A state of "Internal Security Emergency" (hereinafter referred to as the "emergency") so declared shall continue in existence until terminated by proclamation of the President or by concurrent resolution of the Congress. . . .

Sec. 103. (a) Whenever there shall be in existence such an emergency, the President, acting through the Attorney General, is hereby authorized to apprehend and by order detain, pursuant to the provisions of this title, each person as to whom there is reasonable ground to believe that such person probably will engage in, or probably will conspire with others to engage in, acts of espionage or of sabotage. . . .

TRUMAN'S VETO OF THE McCARRAN-WALTER
IMMIGRATION ACT
June 25, 1952

(82nd Congress, 2nd Session, House Doc. No. 520)

The McCarran-Walter Immigration Act continued the basic quota system
of immigration adopted in 1924. It included new provisions to prevent
the admission of possible subversives and to permit the expulsion of
dangerous aliens. President Truman vetoed the bill on constitutional
and other grounds, but Congress passed it over his veto by a vote of
278 to 133 in the House and 57 to 26 in the Senate.

Source: By permission from Documents of American History, Vol. II,
8th Edition, edited by Henry Steele Commager, New York: Appleton-
Century-Crofts, Educational Division, Meredith Corp., 1968.

To the House of Representatives:
        I return herewith, without my approval, H. R. 5678, the proposed
Immigration and Nationality Act.
        In outlining my objections to this bill, I want to make it clear that
it contains certain provisions that meet with my approval. This is a long
and complex piece of legislation. It has 164 separate sections, some
with more that 40 subdivisions. It presents a difficult problem of weigh-
ing the good against the bad, and arriving at a judgment on the whole.
        H. R. 5678 is an omnibus bill which would revise and codify all
of our laws relating to immigration, naturalization, and nationality.
        A general revision and modernization of these laws unquestion-
ably is needed and long overdue, particularly with respect to immigration. But this bill would not provide us with an immigration policy
adequate for the present world situation. Indeed, the bill, taking all
its provisions together, would be a step backward and not a step forward. In view of the crying need for reform in the field of immigration, I deeply regret that I am unable to approve H. R. 5678.
        In recent years our immigration policy has become a matter of
major national concern. Long dormant questions about the effect of
our immigration laws now assume first-rate importance. What we do
in the field of immigration and naturalization is vital to the continued
growth and internal development of the United States -- to the economic
and social strength of our country -- which is the core of the defense
of the free world. Our immigration policy is equally, if not more, important to the conduct of our foreign relations and to our responsibilities of moral leadership in the struggle for world peace.
        In one respect, this bill recognizes the great international sig-
nificance of our immigration and naturalization policy, and takes a step
to improve existing laws. All racial bars to naturalization would be
removed, and at least some minimum immigration quota would be

afforded to each of the free nations of Asia.

I have long urged that racial or national barriers to naturalization be abolished. This was one of the recommendations in my civil-
rights message to the Congress on February 2, 1948. On February 19,
1951, the House of Representatives unanimously passed a bill to carry
it out.

But now this most desirable provision comes before me embed-
ded in a mass of legislation which would perpetuate injustices of long
standing against many other nations of the world, hamper the efforts
we are making to rally the men of the east and west alike to the cause
of freedom, and intensify the repressive and inhumane aspects of our
immigration procedures. The price is too high and, in good conscience,
I cannot agree to pay it. . . .

In addition to removing racial bars to naturalization, the bill would
permit American women citizens to bring their alien husbands to this
country as nonquota immigrants, and enable alien husbands of resident
women aliens to come in under the quota in a preferred status. These
provisions would be a step toward preserving the integrity of the family under our immigration laws, and are clearly desirable. . . .

But these few improvements are heavily outweighed by other provisions of the bill which retain existing defects in our laws, and add
many undesirable new features.

The bill would continue, practically without change, the national
origins quota system, which was enacted into law in 1924, and put into
effect in 1929. This quota system -- always based upon assumptions at
variance with our American ideals -- is long since out of date and more
than ever unrealistic in the face of present world conditions.

This system hinders us in dealing with current immigration problems, and is a constant handicap in the conduct of our foreign relations.
As I stated in my message to Congress on March 24, 1952, on the need
for an emergency program of immigration from Europe:

> "Our present quota system is not only inadequate to meet
> present emergency needs, it is also an obstacle to the develop-
> ment of an enlightened and satisfactory immigration policy for
> the long-run future."

The inadequacy of the present quota system has been demonstrated since the end of the war, when we were compelled to resort to emergency legislation to admit displaced persons. If the quota system remains unchanged, we shall be compelled to resort to similar emergency legislation again, in order to admit any substantial portion of
the refugees from communism or the victims of overcrowding in Europe.

With the idea of quotas in general there is no quarrel. Some nu-
merical limitations must be set, so that immigration will be within our
capacity to absorb. But the over-all limitation of numbers imposed by
the national origins quota system is too small for our needs today, and
the country by country limitations create a pattern that is insulting to
large numbers of our finest citizens, irritating to our allies abroad,
and foreign to our purposes and ideals.

The over-all quota limitation, under the law of 1924, restricted
annual immigration to approximately 150,000. This was about one-

seventh of 1 percent of our total population in 1920. Taking into account
the growth in population since 1920, the law now allows us but one-
tenth of 1 percent of our total population. And since the largest national
quotas are only partly used, the number actually coming in has been
in the neighborhood of one-fifteenth of 1 percent. This is far less than we
must have in the years ahead to keep up with the growing needs of our
Nation for manpower to maintain the strength and vigor of our economy.

The greatest vice of the present quota system, however, is that
it discriminates, deliberately and intentionally, against many of the
peoples of the world. The purpose behind it was to cut down and virtually eliminate immigration to this country from southern and eastern
Europe. A theory was invented to rationalize this objective. The theory
was that in order to be readily assimilable, European immigrants
should be admitted in proportion to the numbers of persons of their
respective national stocks already here as shown by the census of 1920.
Since Americans of English, Irish, and German descent were most numerous, immigrants of those three nationalities got the lion's share --
more than two-thirds -- of the total quota. The remaining third was
divided up among all the other nations given quotas.

The desired effect was obtained. Immigration from the newer
sources of Southern and Eastern Europe was reduced to a trickle. The
quotas allotted to England and Ireland remained largely unused, as was
intended. Total quota immigration fell to a half or a third -- and some-
times even less -- of the annual limit of 154,000. People from such
countries as Greece, or Spain, or Latvia were virtually deprived of any
opportunity to come here at all, simply because Greeks or Spaniards
or Latvians had not come here before 1920 in any substantial numbers.

The idea behind this discriminatory policy was, to put it baldly,
that Americans with English or Irish names were better people and
better citizens than Americans with Italian or Greek or Polish names.
It was thought that people of West European origin made better citizens
than Rumanians or Yugoslavs or Ukrainians or Hungarians or Balts
or Austrians. Such a concept is utterly unworthy of our traditions and
our ideals. It violates the great political doctrine of the Declaration of
Independence that "all men are created equal." It denies the humanitarian creed inscribed beneath the Statute of Liberty proclaiming to all
nations, "Give me your tired, your poor, your huddled masses yearn-
ing to breathe free."

It repudiates our basic religious concepts, our belief in the brother-
hood of man, and in the words of St. Paul that "there is neither Jew nor
Greek, there is neither bond nor free. . . for ye are all one in Christ
Jesus."

The basis of this quota system was false and unworthy in 1924.
It is even worse now. At the present time this quota system keeps out
the very people we want to bring in. It is incredible to me that, in this
year of 1952, we should again be enacting into law such a slur on the
patriotism, the capacity and the decency of a large part of our cit-
izenry. . . .

The time to shake off this dead weight of past mistakes is now.
The time to develop a decent policy of immigration -- a fitting instru-

ment for our foreign policy and a true reflection of the ideals we stand for, at home and abroad -- is now. In my earlier message on immigration, I tried to explain to the Congress that the situation we face in immigration is an emergency -- that it must be met promptly. I have pointed out that in the last few years we have blazed a new trail in immigration, through our displaced persons program. Through the combined efforts of the Government and private agencies, working together not to keep people out, but to bring qualified people in, we summoned our resources of good will and human feeling to meet the task. In this program we have found better techniques to meet the immigration problems of the 1950's.

None of this fruitful experience of the last 3 years is reflected in this bill before me. None of the crying human needs of this time of trouble is recognized in this bill. But it is not too late. The Congress can remedy these defects, and it can adopt legislation to meet the most critical problems before adjournment. . . .

I now wish to turn to the other provisions of the bill, those dealing with the qualifications of aliens and immigrants for admission, with the administration of the laws, and with problems of naturalization and nationality. In these provisions, too, I find objections that preclude my signing this bill.

The bill would make it even more difficult to enter our country. Our resident aliens would be more easily separated from homes and families under grounds of deportation, both new and old, which would specifically be made retroactive. Admission to our citizenship would be made more difficult; expulsion from our citizenship would be made easier. Certain rights of native-born, first-generation Americans would be limited. All our citizens returning from abroad would be subjected to serious risk of unreasonable invasions of privacy. Seldom has a bill exhibited the distrust evidenced here for citizens and aliens alike -- at a time when we need unity at home and the confidence of our friends abroad. . . .

I am asked to approve the reenactment of highly objectionable provisions now contained in the Internal Security Act of 1950 -- a measure passed over my veto shortly after the invasion of South Korea. Some of these provisions would empower the Attorney General to deport any alien who has engaged or has had a purpose to engage in activities "prejudicial to the public interest" or "subversive to the national security." No standards or definitions are provided to guide discretion in the exercise of powers so sweeping. To punish undefined "activities" departs from traditional American insistence on established standards of guilt. To punish an undefined "purpose" is thought control.

These provisions are worse than the infamous Alien Act of 1798, passed in a time of national fear and distrust of foreigners, which gave the President power to deport any alien deemed "dangerous to the peace and safety of the United States." Alien residents were thoroughly frightened and citizens much disturbed by that threat to liberty.

Such powers are inconsistent with our democratic ideals. Conferring powers like that upon the Attorney General is unfair to him as well as to our alien residents. Once fully informed of such vast discretionary powers vested in the Attorney General, Americans now would and should be just as alarmed as Americans were in 1798 over less drastic powers vested in the President.

Heretofore, for the most part, deportation and exclusion have rested upon findings of fact made upon evidence. Under this bill, they would rest in many instances upon the "opinion" or "satisfaction" of immigration or consular employees. The change from objective findings to subjective feelings is not compatible with our system of justice. The result would be to restrict or eliminate judicial review of unlawful administrative action. . . .

Many of the aspects of the bill which have been most widely criticized in the public debate are reaffirmations or elaborations of existing statutes or administrative procedures. Time and again, examination discloses that the revisions of existing law that would be made by the bill are intended to solidify some restrictive practice of our immigration authorities, or to overrule or modify some ameliorative decision of the Supreme Court or other Federal courts. By and large, the changes that would be made by the bill do not depart from the basically restrictive spirit of our existing laws -- but intensify and reinforce it.

These conclusions point to an underlying condition which deserves the most careful study. Should we not undertake a reassessment of our immigration policies and practices in the light of the conditions that face us in the second half of the twentieth century? The great popular interest which this bill has created, and the criticism which it has stirred up, demand an affirmative answer. I hope the Congress will agree to a careful reexamination of this entire matter. . . .

Harry S Truman.

CALIFORNIA LEGISLATURE ASSEMBLY
RULES COMMITTEE RESOLUTION 310
April 24, 1969

By the Honorable Willie L. Brown, Jr., of the Eighteenth District and the Honorable John L. Burton of the Twentieth District

Relative to the
27th anniversary of the Japanese-American evacuation

WHEREAS, As a result of the war hysteria and racial discrimination prevalent in the spring of 1942, some twenty-seven years ago, exceptionally restrictive measures were summarily taken against American citizens of Japanese ancestry; and

WHEREAS, Over 100,000 Japanese were removed pursuant to federal orders to inland relocation centers where they were forced to remain for as long as three years; and

WHEREAS, The property loss of the evacuees was estimated by the Federal Reserve Bank of San Francisco as in excess of 400 million dollars, however, the United States Government reimbursed them for less than 10 percent of that amount; and

WHEREAS, No evidence has ever been produced of disloyalty, sabotage, espionage, or any overt acts which would justify such summary removal and dislocation; and

WHEREAS, Japanese volunteers later served with distinction and valor in the armed forces of the United States in World War II on every battlefront; and

WHEREAS, Americans of Japanese ancestry, after their return to the coastal cities and towns of California, recovered from their incarceration and vast property losses and have made tremendous progress in economic, social, and political areas; now, therefore, be it

Resolved by the Assembly Rules Committee, That the Members commend the Japanese-Americans of California and the United States for their unyielding faith in the United States of America and their triumph over wartime adversities and express to them the sincere best wishes and friendship of all of their fellow Californians.

Resolution No. 310 approved by the Assembly Rules Committee

CALIFORNIA LEGISLATURE SENATE RESOLUTION
April 24, 1969

The Senate, California Legislature

By Senator George R. Moscone
and Senator Milton Marks

Resolution
of the Senate Rules Committee

Relative to the 27th Anniversary of
the Japanese-American Evacuation.

WHEREAS, Twenty-seven years ago restrictive measures were taken against American citizens of Japanese ancestry as a result of the war hysteria and racial discrimination prevalent in the spring of 1942; and

WHEREAS, Federal orders effected the removal of over 100,000 Japanese to inland relocation centers where they were forced to remain for as long as three years; and

WHEREAS, The Federal Reserve Bank of San Francisco has estimated the property loss of evacuees as in excess of 400 million dollars, for less than 10 percent of which they were reimbursed by the United States Government; and

WHEREAS, There was no evidence of disloyalty, sabotage, espionage, or any overt acts which would justify such summary removal and dislocation, and Japanese volunteers later served with valor in the United States military forces on every battlefront of World War II; and

WHEREAS, Upon their return to coastal cities and towns of California, Americans of Japanese ancestry have recovered from their wartime experience and have attained tremendous progress in economic, social, and political areas; now, therefore, be it

RESOLVED BY THE SENATE RULES COMMITTEE, That the Members express their sincere friendship and good will toward the Japanese-Americans of California and the United States and wish them continuing prosperity and success and commend them for their unyielding faith in America and their triumph over wartime adversities.

Senate Resolution No. 87 adopted April 24, 1969.

LETTER FROM PRESIDENT NIXON ON THE CENTENNIAL OF JAPANESE IMMIGRATION
May 28, 1969

THE WHITE HOUSE
WASHINGTON
May 28, 1969

It is an honor and a privilege for me to mark the one hundredth anniversary of Japanese immigration to the United States by sending warm greetings to all who take part in its observance. Beginning with the early days when emigration of its subjects was made a capital offense by the Japanese Government, the history of the development of Japanese emigration to this country has indeed been encumbered by difficulties -- doubtless portrayals of the unfortunate temper of times now happily long past.

The immigrants from Japan who settled in this country raised civic-minded, law-abiding families, and became doers and leaders in our communities. They have enriched our way of life more than any of us can ever say.

Their industry and integrity, their desire to further their education and develop their talents; their celebrated bravery aptly reflected in the feats of the 442nd Infantry Regimental Combat Team which served so gloriously in the Second World War, their continuing contributions to science and the arts -- for all these, and many more reasons, Americans of all races, creeds and walks of life join in saluting our fellow citizens of Japanese descent.

We sincerely appreciate the great good you have brought to our shores, and we are proud to acknowledge the many benefits we derive from your continuing national service.

(Signed) Richard Nixon

Appendix A

JAPANESE IN THE UNITED STATES, 1940-1970

Census totals for the Japanese in the United States, including Alaska and Hawaii, for the years 1940, 1950, 1960, and 1970 are as follows.

	1970	1960	1950	1940
Alabama............	1,079	500	88	21
Alaska	916	818	n.a.	263
Arizona	2,394	1,501	780	632
Arkansas	587	237	113	3
California	213,280	157,317	84,956	93,717
Colorado	7,831	6,846	5,412	2,734
Connecticut........	1,621	653	254	164
Delaware..........	359	152	14	22
Dist. of Columbia ...	651	900	353	68
Florida............	4,090	1,315	238	154
Georgia	1,836	885	128	31
Hawaii	217,307	203,455	184,611	157,905
Idaho..............	2,255	2,254	1,980	1,191
Illinois	17,299	14,074	11,646	462
Indiana	2,279	1,093	318	29
Iowa	1,009	599	310	29
Kansas............	1,584	519	127	46
Kentucky	1,095	1,362	116	19
Louisiana..........	1,123	774	74	9
Maine	348	343	30	5
Maryland..........	3,733	1,842	289	36
Massachusetts	4,393	1,924	384	158
Michigan	5,221	3,211	1,517	139
Minnesota	2,603	1,726	1,049	51
Mississippi........	461	178	62	1
Missouri	2,382	1,473	527	74
Montana	574	589	524	508
Nebraska..........	1,314	905	619	480
Nevada	1,087	544	382	470
New Hampshire	360	343	30	5
New Jersey	5,681	3,514	1,784	298
New Mexico........	940	930	251	186
New York..........	20,351	8,702	3,893	2,538
North Carolina	2,104	1,265	98	21

	1970	1960	1950	1940
North Dakota......	239	127	61	83
Ohio	5,555	3,135	1,986	163
Oklahoma.........	1,408	749	137	57
Oregon...........	6,843	5,016	3,660	4,071
Pennsylvania	5,461	2,348	1,029	224
Rhode Island	629	192	25	6
South Carolina	826	460	34	33
South Dakota	221	188	56	19
Tennessee	1,160	507	104	12
Texas	6,537	4,053	957	458
Utah	4,713	4,371	4,452	2,210
Vermont..........	134	79	14	3
Virginia	3,500	1,733	193	74
Washington	20,335	16,652	9,694	14,565
West Virginia	368	176	46	3
Wisconsin	2,648	1,425	529	23
Wyoming	566	514	450	643
Japanese (Total)....	591,290	464,468	353,384	285,116

Appendix B
THE ASSEMBLY CENTERS

The following were the initial round-up stations of the West Coast Japanese people where they lived for several months until they were removed to Relocation Centers.

California:
1. Salinas

2. Tanforan Racetrack, San Francisco

3. Turlock

4. Tulare

5. Sacramento

6. Merced

7. Fresno

8. Pinedale

9. Pomona

10. Santa Anita Racetrack, Los Angeles

11. Marysville

12. Stockton

Oregon: Livestock Exposition Hall, Portland

Washington: The Fairgrounds, Puyallup

Arizona: Mayer

Appendix C

THE "RELOCATION CENTERS"

West Coast Japanese Americans were incarcerated in the following "relocation centers" during World War II.

Arizona:
        Gila River
        Poston

Arkansas:
        Jerome
        Rohwer

California:
        Manzanar
        Tule Lake

Colorado:
        Granada

Idaho:
        Minidoka

Utah:
        Topaz

Wyoming:
        Heart Mountain

Appendix D

THE BATTLES FOUGHT BY THE NISEI MEN OF
THE 442nd INFANTRY REGIMENT DURING WORLD WAR II

Volturno River

Rapido River

Cassino

Anzio Beachhead

Hill 140

Belvedere

Sasseta

Luciana

Leghorn

Arno River

Invasion of Southern France

Bruyères

Rescue of the Lost Battalion

Maritime Alps

La Spezia

Massa

Carrara

Genoa

Casualties = 314% of original strength of unit.

Appendix E

INDIVIDUAL AWARDS AND DECORATIONS RECEIVED BY THE NISEI MEN OF THE 442nd INFANTRY REGIMENT OF WORLD WAR II

1 Congressional Medal of Honor

52 Distinguished Service Crosses

1 Distinguished Service Medal

560 Silver Stars

28 Oak Leaf Clusters to the Sliver Star

22 Legions of Merit

15 Soldier's Medals

4,000 (approx.) Bronze Stars

1,200 (approx.) Oak Leaf Clusters to the Bronze Star Medal

12 French Croix de Guerre

2 Palms to the French Croix de Guerre

2 Italian Crosses for Military Merit

2 Italian Medals for Military Valor

7 Presidential Distinguished Unit Citations

2 Meritorious Service Unit Plaques

1 Army Unit Commendation

Appendix F

JAPANESE AMERICAN NEWSPAPERS

California

Los Angeles. Gidra, P.O. Box 18046 (ZIP 90018), monthly
Kashu Mainichi*, 346 E. 1st St. (ZIP 90012),
daily except Sunday
Little Tokyo*, 1709 W. 8th St. (ZIP 90017),
magazine, monthly
Pacific Citizen, 125 Weller St. (ZIP 90012),
weekly
Rafu Shimpo*, 242 S. San Pedro St. (ZIP 90012),
daily, except Sunday

San Francisco. Hokubei Mainichi*, P.O. Box 3321 (ZIP 94119),
daily,except Sunday
Nichibei Times*, P.O. Box 3098 (ZIP 94119),
daily, except Sunday

Colorado   Denver. Rocky Mountain Jiho*, 28 E. 20th Ave.
(ZIP 80202), weekly

Hawaii   Honolulu. Hawaii Hochi*, P.O. Box 1290 (ZIP 96817),
daily, except Sunday
Hawaii Times*, P.O. Box 1230 (ZIP 96817),
daily, except Sunday

Illinois   Chicago. Chicago Shimpo*, 3744 N. Clark St.
(ZIP 60613), biweekly

Utah   Salt Lake City. Utah Nippo*, 52 N. 9th West (ZIP 84116),
triweekly

New York   New York City. New York Nichibei*, 260 W. Broadway
(ZIP 10013), weekly

*Denotes those which include the Japanese vernacular

Appendix G

NISEI SCIENTISTS IN AMERICA

Amemiya, Minoru, Ph.D. soil chemistry, research, Iowa State.
Asano, Akira, Ph.D. pharmacology, assistant director, J & J.
Doi, Roy H., Ph.D. bacteriology, University of California, Davis.
Fukui, George M., Ph.D. microbiology, research, Wallace Laboratories.
Fukui, Henry N., Ph.D. chemistry, professor, Youngstown Ohio College.
Fukui, Paul T., M.D. neurology, V.A. Hospital, Coatesville, Pennsylvania.
Furukawa, David H., research engineer, U.S. Bureau of Reclamation,
            Denver, Colorado.
Hashimoto, Edward C., M.D., anatomy, assistant professor University
            of Utah Medical School.
Hayashi, Teruo, M.D., professor, Ob-Gyn, University of Pittsburgh, Penn-
            sylvania.
Higano, Norio, M.D. internal medicine, Massachusetts.
Higuchi, Takeru, Ph.D., pharmacology, University of Kansas.
Ikawa, Miyoshi, Ph.D., biochemistry, professor, University of New Hamp-
            shire.
Itano, Harvey, M.D., Ph.D., pathology, University of California at San
            Diego School of Medicine.
Ito, Susumu, Ph.D., chemistry, assistant professor Harvard Medical
            School.
Iwasaki, Tets, space scientist, graduate of C.I.T. and M.I.T., with NASA.
Kato, Walter, Ph.D., reactor physics, chief, Argonne National Laborator-
            ies.
Kimura, Kazuo, M.D., pediatrics, pharmacology, Pennsylvania.
Kinoshita, Jin, Ph.D., biochemistry, National Eye Institute.
Konzo, Seichi, Ph.D., mechanical engineer, University of Illinois.
Kubota, Toshi, Ph.D., aeronautical engineer, associate professor C.I.T.
Kudo, Albert M., Ph.D., geology, assistant professor, University of New
            Mexico.
Kurahara, S.S., M.D., Ph.D., radiology, assistant professor, University
            of Southern California
Maruyama, Yosh, M.D., radiation, University of Kansas.
Mayeda, Kaz, Ph.D., genetics, associate professor, Department of Biology
            Wayne State University, Detroit, Michigan.
Moriyama, Iwao Milton, M.D., chief of mortality, analysis section,
            Washington, D.C.
Murakami, William Tsunehisa, Ph.D., biochemistry, Brandeis University,
            Massachusetts.
Murata, Jack, agricultural chemist, Department of Interior, Washington,
            D.C.

Murayama, Makio, Ph.D., biochemistry, National Institutes of Health, Bethesda, Maryland.

Nagamatsu, George Rio, M.D., urologist, surgeon, New York.

Nagamatsu, Henry T., Ph.D., research & development, G.E., Schenectady, New York.

Naka, Robert, D.Sc., electron optics, deputy undersecretary, Department of Air Force.

Okita, George T., Ph.D., pharmacology, professor, Northwestern University

Okura, K. Patrick, director of Nebraska Psychiatric Institute.

Omori, Thomas T., Ph.D., aerospace scientist, Far East manager for International Operations, Aeroject General Corporation, Azusa, California.

Ota, Minol, D.V.M., veterinarian, Lovell, Wyoming.

Oyama, Jiro, Ph.D., NASA, Ames Research Center, California.

Oyama, Vance I., Ph.D., NASA, Ames Research Center, California

Shima, Donald, D.D.S., instructor, Fairleigh Dickinson University.

Shirai, Akira, Ph.D., microbiology, Industrial Biological Lab, research at Walter Reed Hospital, Maryland.

Sugiyama, Hiroshi, Ph.D., bacteriology, professor, University of Wisconsin.

Sunada, Kayo, director of home for mentally retarded.

Susuki, Takeo, invertebrate paleontologist.

Takahashi, William N., Ph.D., plant pathology, professor, University of California at Berkeley.

Takamine, Jokichi, M.D. (grandson of Dr. J. Takamine of adrenalin and diastase fame), Medi-Cal Commission, California

Takehara, Kenneth Nobuaki, Ph.D., biochemist.

Takemori, A.E., Ph.D., pharmacology, University of Minnesota.

Taketa, Tom T., Ph.D., NASA, Ames Research Center, California.

Tamaki, Hitoshi Tom, M.D., pathology, Pennsylvania.

Tashiro, Haruo, Ph.D., entymology, professor, Cornell University, New York.

Terasaki, Paul I., Ph.D., immunology, professor, UCLA School of Medicine.

Tomiyasu, Kiyo, Ph.D., technical director of G.E. Lasen Laboratory, Schenectady, New York.

Tomozawa, Francis, optometrist, California

Tsuchiya, Henry M., Ph.D., microbiology, professor, University of Minnesota.

Tsuji, Frederick Ichiro, Ph.D., biochemistry, Pennsylvania.

Tsunoda, Kenneth, B.S., M.I.T., engineer.

Uyehara, Otto A., Ph.D., mechanical engineer, professor, University of Wisconsin.

Wakamatsu, Shigeo, chemist, Lever Brothers, New York.

Watanabe, Warren, Ph.D., chemistry, research, Rohm and Haas.

Wesley (Uyesugi) Newton, pioneer researcher in contact lenses.

Yamauchi, Thomas T., chief of systems engineering and technology on Lunar Orbiter Program, Viking Program Engineer for Boeing.

Yamazaki, William T., Ph.D., agronomy, professor, Ohio State University.
Yokoyama, Katsuyuki, Ph.D., NASA, Ames Research Center, California.
Yoshida, Yutaka Ronald, B.S., M.S., M.I.T., mechanical engineering,
                        C.I.T., Jet Propulsion Laboratory, Pasadena,
                        California.

Appendix H

JAPAN-BORN SCIENTISTS IN AMERICA

Esaki, Leo, Ph.D. physicist, IBM, New York.
Fukui, Hatsuaki, D. Eng., engineer, vice president, Sony Corporation of
America, p.a. New York.
Hara, Hatsuji J., M.D., otolaryngology, clinical professor, Loma Linda
University, California.
Hayatsu, Ryochi, Ph.D., organic chemistry, research assistant, Univer-
sity of Chicago.
Igusa, Junichi, Ph.D., mathematician, educator, professor Johns Hopkins
University, Maryland.
Inoue, Shinya, Ph.D., educator, (b. England), p.a. Pennsylvania.
Ishii, Thomas K., Ph.D., electrical engineering, professor Marquette
University College of Engineering, Illionois.
Ishizaka, Kimishige, M.D., immunologist, professor Johns Hopkins Medi-
cal School, Maryland.
Ito, Kiyoshi, Ph.D., Cornell University, New York.
Iwasawa, Kenkichi, D.Sc., mathematician, professor M.I.T. and Prince-
ton.
Kasaga, Kazumi, M.D., specialist in TB control, U.S. Public Health Ser-
vice, Washington, D.C.
Kikuchi, Chihiro, Ph.D., mathematician, physicist, atomic engineer, fa-
culty of University of Michigan, Ann Arbor, Michigan.
Kinoshita, Jin, M.D., ophthalmologist pioneer, (sugar cataracts).
Kinoshita, Riojun, M.D., pathology director, City of Hope Medical Center,
Duarte, California.
Kinoshita, Toichiro, Ph.D., physicist, p.a. New York.
Kubota, Tomio, D.Sc., mathematician, University of Maryland.
Kudo, Richard R., D.Sc., zoology professor emeritus, University of South-
ern Illinois.
Kuroda, Paul K., Ph.D., chemistry, professor, University of Arkansas,
Fayetteville, Arkansas.
Manabe, Syukuro, D.Sc., meteorology, research, Environmental Science
Service, Washington, D.C.
Masubuchi, Koichi, Ph.D., naval architect, M.I.T.
Matsumura, Fumio, Ph.D., entymology, assistant professor, University of
Wisconsin.
Mikuriya, Tadafumi, civil structural engineer, p.a. New Jersey
Myoda, Timothy, Ph.D., microbiology, research, Nemours Institute.
Noguchi, Thomas T., M.D., pathology, assistant professor, Loma Linda
University, California.

Ooyama, Katsuyaki, Ph.D., meteorologist, educator, p.a. New York.

Shibutani, Kinichi, M.D., anesthesiologist, Grasslands Hospital, Valhalla, New York.

Shinya, Hiromi, M.D., chief of surgical endoscopy unit, Beth Israel Medical Center, New York, assistant professor of surgery, Mount Sinai School of Medicine, New York.

Sueoki, Noboru, Ph.D., biochemistry, assistant professor, Princeton, New Jersey.

Tokuhata, George K., Ph.D., director of research, Pennsylvania Department of Health, p.a. Pennsylvania.

Tsutsui, Minoru, D.Sc., organic chemistry, assistant professor, N.Y.U.

Tutihasi, Simpei, D.Sc., physicist, Xerox Corporation, New York.

Yagi, Yasuo, D.Sc., chemistry, assistant professor, State University of New York at Buffalo.

Yukawa, Hideki, physicist, Nobel Prize winner in physics for meson theory, Japan.

b. = born in
p.a. = present address

Appendix I

JAPANESE IN AMERICA LISTED IN WHO'S WHO IN THE EAST,
14th EDITION 1974-1975

Fukui, Hatsuaki - D.Eng., executive, electronics company, b. Japan 1927,
      New York
Hayashi, Teruo Terry - M.D., Ob-Gyn., b. U.S.A. 1921.
Higano, Norio - M.D., b. U.S.A. 1921.
Igusa, Junichi - Mathematician, educator, b. Japan 1924.
Inagaki, Morido - economist, educator, b. Japan 1923, Canada.
Inoue, Shinya - educator, b. England 1921.
Ishikawa, Samuel - business executive, b. U.S.A. 1922, New York.
Ito, Kiyoshi - educator, mathematician, b. Japan 1915, New York.
Iwasawa, Kenkichi - mathematician, b. Japan 1917, New Jersey.
Kako, Takashi - broadcasting executive, b. U.S.A 1927, New York.
Kimura, Kazuo - M.D., chemical company executive, b. U.S.A 1920,
            Pennsylvania.
Kinoshita, Toichiro - physicist, educator, b. Japan 1925, New York.
Kubota, Tomio - D.Sc., educator, mathematician, b. Japan 1930, Maryland.
Kurihara, Kenneth Kenkichi - economist, educator, b. Japan 1910, New York.
Masubuchi, Koichi - naval architect, b. Japan 1924, Massachusetts.
Mikuriya, Tadafumi - civil structural engineer, b. Japan 1899, Pennsylvania.
Mizuno, Ikuko - violinist, b. Japan 1942, Massachusetts.
Murakami, William Tsunehisa - Ph.D., educator, biochemist, b. U.S.A.
                  1928, Massachusetts.
Murasugi, Kunio - educator, b. Japan 1929, Canada.
Nagamatsu, George Rio - M.D., urologist, surgeon, b. U.S.A. 1904, New
                  York.
Naito, Takeshi - investment banker, b. Japan 1929, New York.
Ninomiya, Yumi (Mrs. Henry G. Scott) - violinist, b. Japan 1943, Pennsyl-
                        vania.
Nishimoto, Kenichi - government official, b. U.S.A. 1913, Maryland.
Nishizaki, Shunya Thomas - foreign trade company executive, b. U.S.A.
                  1926, New York.
Oi, Walter Yasuo - Ph.D., educator, economist, b. U.S.A. 1929, New
                  York.
Okada, Kenzo - artist, b. Japan 1902, New York.
Ooyama, Katsuyuki - Ph.D., educator, meteorologist, b. Japan 1929, New
                  York.
Sato, Kazuo - Ph.D., economist, educator, b. Japan 1927, New York.
Shibutani, Kinichi - M.D., b. Japan 1927, anesthesiology, New York.
Shima, Donald - D.D.S., b. U.S.A. 1935, New Jersey
Takehara, Kenneth Nobuaki - Ph.D., biochemist, b. U.S.A. 1923, Maryland.

Tamaki, Hitoshi Tom - M.D., pathologist, b. U.S.A. 1917, Pennsylvania.
Tokita, Ryotaro - painter, printmaker, b. Japan 1930, New York.
Tokuhata, George Kazunari - Ph.D., educator, health scientist, b. Japan
　　　　　　　　　　　1924, Pennsylvania.
Tsuji, Frederick Ichiro - Ph.D., biochemist, educator, b. U.S.A. 1923,
　　　　　　　　　　　Pennsylvania.
Tsunoda, Kenneth - B.S. M.I.T., engineer, company executive, b. U.S.A.
　　　　　　　　　　　1920, New Jersey.
Tutihasi, Simpei - D.Sc., physicist, b. Japan 1922, New York.
Watanabe, Ruth - librarian, b. U.S.A. 1916, New York.
Yoshida, Okiru - social worker, b. U.S.A. 1933, New York.

b. = born in

Appendix J

NONWHITE POPULATION, BY SEX AND RACE, 1820-1950

Source: Historical Statistics of the United States, Colonial Times to 1957, A Statistical Abstract Supplement. U.S. Department of Commerce Bureau of the Census with the Cooperation of the Social Science Research Council.

Year	Male					
	Negro [1]		Indian	Japanese	Chinese	All other
	Total	Slave				
	59	60	61	62	63	64
1950	7,298,722	----------	178,824	76,649	77,008	[2]72,844
1940	6,269,038	----------	171,427	71,967	57,389	43,223
1930	5,855,669	----------	170,350	81,771	59,802	46,960
1920	5,209,436	----------	125,068	72,707	53,891	8,674
1910	4,885,881	----------	135,133	63,070	66,856	3,092
1900	4,386,547	----------	119,484	23,341	85,341	----------
1890	3,735,603	----------	125,719	1,780	103,620	----------
1880	3,253,115	----------	[3]33,985	134	100,686	----------
1870	[4]2,393,263	----------	[3]12,534	47	58,633	----------
1860	2,216,744	1,982,625	[3]23,924	----------	33,149	----------
1850	1,811,258	1,602,535	----------	----------	----------	----------
1840	1,432,988	1,246,467	----------	----------	----------	----------
1830	1,166,276	1,012,823	----------	----------	----------	----------
1820	898,892	786,022	----------	----------	----------	----------

Year	Female					
	Negro [1]		Indian	Japanese	Chinese	All other
	Total	Slave				
	65	66	67	68	69	70
1950	7,743,564	----------	164,586	65,119	40,621	[2]37,396
1940	6,596,480	----------	162,542	54,980	20,115	7,244
1930	6,035,474	----------	162,047	57,063	15,152	4,018
1920	5,253,695	----------	119,369	38,303	7,748	814
1910	4,941,882	----------	130,550	9,087	4,675	83
1900	4,447,447	----------	117,712	985	4,522	----------
1890	3,753,073	----------	122,534	259	3,868	----------
1880	3,327,678	----------	[3]32,422	14	4,779	----------
1870	[4]2,486,746	----------	[3]13,197	8	4,566	----------
1860	2,225,086	1,971,135	[3]20,097	----------	1,784	----------
1850	1,827,550	1,601,778	----------	----------	----------	----------
1840	1,440,660	1,240,888	----------	----------	----------	----------
1830	1,162,866	996,220	----------	----------	----------	----------
1820	872,764	752,000	----------	----------	----------	----------

[1] Sex not reported before 1820. Total for both sexes from 1790 to 1810 is as follows: For 1810, total 1,377,808, slaves 1,191,362; 1800, total 1,002,037, slaves 893,602; and 1790, total 757,208, slaves 697,681.
[2] Includes persons of mixed white, Negro, and Indian ancestry in certain communities in eastern United States.

[3] Excludes Indians in Indian Territory and on Indian reservations.
[4] Adjustment for underenumeration in Southern States shows 5,392,172 Negroes for both sexes combined.

Appendix K

IMMIGRANTS, BY COUNTRY, 1820-1957

Source: <u>Historical Statistics of the United States, Colonial Times to 1957, A Statistical Abstract Supplement</u>. U.S. Department of Commerce Bureau of the Census with the Cooperation of the Social Science Research Council.

Year	Asia				
	Total	Turkey in Asia [1]	China	Japan [2]	Other Asia [3]
	101	102	103	104	105
1957	20,008	77	2,098	6,829	11,004
1956	17,327	48	1,386	5,967	9,926
1955	10,935	54	568	4,150	6,163
1954	9,970	33	254	3,846	5,837
1953	8,231	13	528	2,579	5,111
1952	9,328	12	263	3,814	5,239
1951	3,921	3	335	271	3,312
1950	3,779	13	1,280	100	2,386
1949	6,438	40	3,415	529	2,454
1948	10,739	16	7,203	423	3,097
1947	5,823	22	3,191	131	2,479
1946	1,633	16	252	14	1,351
1945	442	13	71	1	357
1944	227	15	50	4	158
1943	334	36	65	20	213
1942	564	31	179	44	310
1941	1,801	16	1,003	289	493
1940	1,913	7	643	102	1,161
1939	2,162	15	642	102	1,403
1938	2,376	11	613	93	1,659
1937	1,065	13	293	132	627
1936	721	20	273	91	337
1935	682	31	229	88	334
1934	597	22	187	86	302
1933	552	27	148	75	302
1932	1,931	43	750	526	612
1931	3,345	139	1,150	653	1,403
1930	4,535	118	1,589	837	1,991
1929	3,758	70	1,446	771	1,471
1928	3,380	80	1,320	550	1,430
1927	3,669	73	1,471	723	1,402
1926	3,413	37	1,751	654	971
1925	3,578	51	1,937	723	867
1924	22,065	2,820	6,992	8,801	3,452
1923	13,705	2,183	4,986	5,809	727
1922	14,263	1,998	4,406	6,716	1,143
1921	25,034	11,735	4,009	7,878	1,412
1920	17,505	5,033	2,330	9,432	710
1919	12,674	19	1,964	10,064	627
1918	12,701	43	1,795	10,213	650
1917	12,756	393	2,237	8,991	1,135
1916	13,204	1,670	2,460	8,680	394
1915	15,211	3,543	2,660	8,613	395
1914	34,273	21,716	2,502	8,929	1,126
1913	35,358	23,955	2,105	8,281	1,017
1912	21,449	12,788	1,765	6,114	782
1911	17,428	10,229	1,460	4,520	1,219

[1] No record of immigration from Turkey in Asia until 1869.
[2] No record of immigration from Japan until 1861.
[3] Philippine Islands are included in "Other Asia" in 1952 (1,179), 1953 (1,074), 1954 (1,234), 1955 (1,598), 1956 (1,792), and 1957 (1,874). From 1934 to 1951, inclusive, they are included in "All other countries."

Year	Asia				
	Total	Turkey in Asia [1]	China	Japan [2]	Other Asia [3]
	101	102	103	104	105
1910	23,533	15,212	1,968	2,720	3,633
1909	12,904	7,506	1,943	3,111	344
1908	28,365	9,753	1,397	15,803	1,412
1907	40,524	8,053	961	30,226	1,284
1906	22,300	6,354	1,544	13,835	567
1905	23,925	6,157	2,166	10,331	5,271
1904	26,186	5,235	4,309	14,264	2,378
1903	29,966	7,118	2,209	19,968	671
1902	22,271	6,223	1,649	14,270	129
1901	13,593	5,782	2,459	5,269	83
1900	17,946	3,962	1,247	12,635	102
1899	8,972	4,436	1,660	2,844	32
1898	8,637	4,275	2,071	2,230	61
1897	9,662	4,732	3,363	1,526	41
1896	6,764	4,139	1,441	1,110	74
1895	4,495	2,767	539	1,150	39
1894	4,690	---------	1,170	1,931	1,589
1893	2,392		472	1,380	540
1892					
1891	7,678	2,488	2,836	1,136	1,218
1890	4,448	1,126	1,716	691	915
1889	1,725	593	118	640	874
1888	843	273	26	404	140
1887	615	208	10	229	168
1886	317	15	40	194	68
1885	198	---------	22	49	127
1884	510		279	20	211
1883	8,113		8,031	27	55
1882	39,629		39,579	5	45
1881	11,982	5	11,890	11	76
1880	5,839	4	5,802	4	29
1879	9,660	31	9,604	4	21
1878	9,014	7	8,992	2	13
1877	10,640	3	10,594	7	36
1876	22,943	8	22,781	4	150
1875	16,499	1	16,437	3	58
1874	13,838	6	13,776	21	35
1873	20,325	3	20,292	9	21
1872	7,825	---------	7,788	17	20
1871	7,240	4	7,135	78	23
1870	15,825	---------	15,740	48	37
1869	12,949	2	12,874	63	10
1868	5,171	---------	5,157	---------	14
1867	3,961	---------	3,863	67	31
1866	2,411	---------	2,385	7	19

[1] No record of immigration from Turkey in Asia until 1869.
[2] No record of immigration from Japan until 1861.
[3] Philippine Islands are included in "Other Asia" in 1952 (1,179), 1953 (1,074), 1954 (1,234), 1955 (1,598), 1956 (1,792), and 1957 (1,874). From 1934 to 1951, inclusive, they are included in "All other countries."

Year	Asia				
	Total	Turkey in Asia[1]	China	Japan[2]	Other Asia[3]
	101	102	103	104	105
1865	2,947		2,942		5
1864	2,982		2,975		7
1863	7,216		7,214		2
1862	3,640		3,633		7
1861	7,528		7,518	1	9
1860	5,476		5,467		9
1859	3,461		3,457		4
1858	5,133		5,128		5
1857	5,945		5,944		1
1856	4,747		4,733		14
1855	3,540		3,526		14
1854	13,100		13,100		
1853	47		42		5
1852	4				4
1851	2				2
1850	7		3		4
1849	11		3		8
1848	8				8
1847	12		4		8
1846	11		7		4
1845	6		6		
1844	6		3		3
1843	11		3		8
1842	7		4		3
1841	3		2		1
1840	1				1
1839					
1838	1				1
1837	11				11
1836	4				4
1835	17		8		9
1834	6				6
1833	3				3
1832	4				4
1831	1				1
1830					
1829	2		1		1
1828	3				3
1827	1				1
1826	1				1
1825	1		1		
1824	1				1
1823					
1822	1				1
1821					
1820	5		1		4

[1] No record of immigration from Turkey in Asia until 1869.
[2] No record of immigration from Japan until 1861.
[3] Philippine Islands are included in "Other Asia" in 1952 (1,179), 1953 (1,074), 1954 (1,234), 1955 (1,598), 1956 (1,792), and 1957 (1,874). From 1934 to 1951, inclusive, they are included in "All other countries."

Appendix L

POPULATION, BY RACE AND SEX, 1940-1970
AND URBAN-RURAL RESIDENCE, 1960 AND 1970

[In thousands. Prior to 1960, excludes Alaska and Hawaii. For complete census count, see tables 32 and 40. See also *Historical Statistics, Colonial Times to 1957*, series A34-70]

RACE AND SEX	1940	1950	1960			1970		
			Total	Urban [1]	Rural [1]	Total	Urban [1]	Rural [1]
Total	131,669	150,697	179,323	125,268	54,054	203,212	149,325	53,887
White	118,215	134,942	158,832	110,428	48,403	177,749	128,773	48,976
Negro	12,866	15,042	18,872	13,808	5,064	22,580	18,367	4,213
Indian	334	343	524	146	378	793	356	437
Japanese	127	142	464	381	83	591	524	68
Chinese	77	118	237	227	11	435	419	16
Filipino	46	62	176	130	47	343	293	50
Other [2]	5	49	218	150	68	721	593	132
Male	66,062	74,833	88,331	60,733	27,598	98,912	71,959	26,954
White	59,449	67,129	78,367	53,631	24,736	86,721	62,210	24,511
Negro	6,269	7,299	9,113	6,557	2,556	10,748	8,657	2,091
Indian	171	179	263	72	191	389	172	217
Japanese	72	77	225	184	41	271	240	31
Chinese	57	77	136	129	6	229	220	8
Filipino	40	46	112	80	32	189	159	31
Other [2]	4	27	115	79	36	365	300	64
Female	65,608	75,864	90,992	64,536	26,456	104,300	77,366	26,933
White	58,766	67,813	80,465	56,797	23,667	91,028	66,563	24,465
Negro	6,596	7,744	9,758	7,251	2,508	11,832	9,710	2,122
Indian	163	165	260	74	187	404	184	220
Japanese	55	65	240	197	43	320	283	37
Chinese	20	41	102	97	4	206	199	8
Filipino	6	16	64	50	14	154	134	19
Other [2]	1	22	103	71	33	356	293	63

[1] Based on 1960 urban definition; see text, p. 2.

[2] Aleuts, Asian Indians, Eskimos, Hawaiians, Indonesians, Koreans, Polynesians, and other races not shown separately.

Source: U.S. Bureau of the Census, *U.S. Census of Population: 1950*, vol. II, part 1, and vol. IV, part 3; *1960*: vol. I; and *1970*, *General Population Characteristics*, final report, PC (1)- B1, *United States Summary*.

Appendix M

POPULATION OF RACES OTHER THAN WHITE OR NEGRO, BY STATES, 1970

STATE	Indian	Japa-nese	Chi-nese	Fili-pino	All other [1]	STATE	Indian	Japa-nese	Chi-nese	Fili-pino	All other [1]
U.S.	792,730	591,290	435,062	343,060	720,520	Mo.	5,405	2,382	2,815	2,010	6,222
						Mont.	27,130	574	289	236	1,142
Ala.	2,443	1,079	626	540	2,179	Nebr.	6,624	1,314	551	324	1,902
Alaska	16,276	916	228	1,498	35,786	Nev.	7,933	1,087	955	817	2,007
Ariz.	95,812	2,394	3,878	1,253	9,271	N.H.	361	360	420	157	772
Ark.	2,014	587	743	289	1,302	N.J.	4,706	5,681	9,233	5,623	22,721
Calif.	91,018	213,280	170,131	138,859	178,671	N. Mex.	72,788	940	563	386	5,953
Colo.	8,836	7,831	1,489	1,068	9,272	N.Y.	28,355	20,351	81,378	14,279	89,565
Conn.	2,222	1,621	2,209	2,177	6,845	N.C.	44,406	2,104	1,255	905	5,144
Del.	656	359	559	392	1,403	N. Dak.	14,369	239	165	204	805
D.C.	956	651	2,582	1,662	3,675	Ohio	6,654	5,555	5,305	3,490	13,539
Fla.	6,677	4,090	3,133	5,092	9,457	Okla.	98,468	1,408	999	612	5,488
Ga.	2,347	1,836	1,584	1,253	4,164	Oreg.	13,510	6,843	4,814	1,633	6,198
Hawaii	1,126	217,307	52,039	93,915	98,441	Pa.	5,533	5,461	7,053	4,560	17,056
Idaho	6,687	2,255	498	206	1,989	R.I.	1,390	629	1,093	1,761	1,757
Ill.	11,413	17,299	14,474	12,654	32,081	S.C.	2,241	826	521	1,222	2,235
Ind.	3,887	2,279	2,115	1,365	6,235	S. Dak.	32,365	221	163	83	715
Iowa	2,992	1,009	993	614	3,410	Tenn.	2,276	1,160	1,610	846	2,604
Kans.	8,672	1,584	1,233	758	5,286	Texas	17,957	6,537	7,635	3,442	45,026
Ky.	1,531	1,095	558	612	2,351	Utah	11,273	4,713	1,281	392	3,071
La.	5,294	1,123	1,340	1,249	3,970	Vt.	229	134	173	53	427
Maine	2,195	348	206	453	770	Va.	4,853	3,500	2,805	7,496	6,958
Md.	4,239	3,733	6,520	5,170	8,370	Wash.	33,386	20,335	9,201	11,462	12,422
Mass.	4,475	4,393	14,012	2,361	10,488	W. Va.	751	368	373	722	1,201
Mich.	16,854	5,221	6,407	3,657	18,404	Wis.	18,924	2,648	2,700	1,209	5,067
Minn.	23,128	2,603	2,422	1,456	4,456	Wyo.	4,980	566	292	108	878
Miss.	4,113	461	1,441	475	1,369						

[1] See footnote 2, table 31.

Source: U.S. Bureau of the Census, *U.S. Census of Population: 1970*, vol. I.

Appendix N

ASIAN ORGANIZATIONS OF THE UNITED STATES, 1973

Recently many Orientals have exhibited a consciousness of other Asian minority groups. As a result of this recent trend many organizations have been born that include Japanese Americans.

LOS ANGELES

JACS-Asian Involvement
    125 Weller St., Room 305
    Los Angeles, CA 90012

Oriental Service Center
    1215 S. Flower St.
    Los Angeles, CA 90012

The Storefront
    2826 W. Jefferson Blvd.
    Los Angeles, CA 90018

Chinatown Youth Council
    971 Chungking Rd.
    Los Angeles, CA 90012

SIPA-Search to Involve
    Philipino-Americans
    c/o 2959 Somerset Dr., L.A. 90016
    or 642 N. Lucerne Blvd., L.A.90004

Amerasia Bookstore
    313½ E. First St.
    Los Angeles, CA 90012

Asian American Studies Center
    3232 Campbell Hall
    University of California, Los Angeles
    Los Angeles, CA 90024

Ethno-Communications
    3232 Campbell Hall, UCLA
    Los Angeles, CA 90024

Visual Communications
    3222 W. Jefferson Blvd.
    Los Angeles, CA 90018

Filipino Community Action Services
    3120 W. 6th St.
    Los Angeles, CA 90020

Filipino Youth Circle
    Los Angeles City College
    855 N. Vermont Ave.
    Los Angeles, CA 90029

SULU (Pilipino Teatro, Arts)
    c/o Lu Pree
    Inner City Theater
    1615 W. Washington Blvd.
    Los Angeles, CA 90007

Asian Social Services Task Force
    c/o 5329 Dockweiler Place
    Los Angeles, CA 90019

Asian American Social Workers
    2400 S. Western Avenue
    Los Angeles, CA 90018

United Samoan Organization
    21224 S. Figueroa
    Carson, CA 90745

Asian Americans for Peace
    c/o P.O. Box 18046
    Los Angeles, CA 90018

Asian American Affirmative Action Comm
   1215 Flower St.
   Los Angeles, CA 90012

Pasadena Asian Community Involvement
   c/o 595 Lincoln Ave.
   Room 203
   Pasadena, CA 91103

Los Angeles Pioneer Center
   125 Weller St., Room 100
   Los Angeles, CA 90012

Southbay Asian Involvement
   16408 S. Western Avenue
   Gardena, CA 90247

Asian American Student Alliance
   3232 Campbell Hall, UCLA
   Los Angeles, CA 90024

Involve Together Asians
   c/o 2110 Barry Ave.
   Los Angeles, CA 90025

Go For Broke
   2420 E. 4th St.
   Los Angeles, CA 90033

Storefront Draft Counseling
   2826 W. Jefferson Blvd.
   Los Angeles, CA 90018

Asian American Student Alliance
   University of Southern California
   681 W. 34th St.
   Los Angeles, CA 90007

Asian American Legal Services
   Legal Aid Foundation
   1112 W. Santa Barbara
   Los Angeles, CA 90037
   (213) 294-6122

PUBLICATIONS

Amerasia Journal
   c/o Asian American Studies Center
   University of California, Los Angeles
   Los Angeles, CA 90024

Chinese Awareness
   971 Chungking Rd.
   Los Angeles, CA 90012

GIDRA
   P.O. Box 18046
   Los Angeles, CA 90018
   (213) 734-7838

SOUTHERN CALIFORNIA

United Asians
   UC Irvine
   c/o Nancy Kikuchi
   370 Avocado St., Apt. 1
   Costa Mesa, CA 92627

Asian American Student Center
   Cal State Long Beach
   6101 E. 7th
   Long Beach, CA 90801

Asian American Student Alliance
   UC San Diego
   Bldg. 250 Mattews Campus
   La Jolla, CA 92037

Asian American Alliance
   UC Santa Barbara
   Box 13462
   Santa Barbara, CA 93107

Mafila
  c/o Art Bigornia
  145 Pacheco
  Vallejo, CA 94590

Apolonario Midini Chapter
UC San Diego
La Jolla, CA 92037

SAN DIEGO

Asian American Drug Education
  Project
  3260 53rd St.
  San Diego, CA 92105

Asian Students
  Morse High School
  281 Flowerdale Lane
  San Diego, CA 92114

United Asian American Community
  c/o Minoru Furuyama
  5716 Hardy Ave.
  San Diego, CA 92115

Ad Hoc Committee on Pilipinos
Student Community Affairs
Andres Bonifacio Chapter
San Diego State College
San Diego, CA 92115

Asian American Student Alliance
  UC San Diego
  c/o Phyllis Chu
  4450 Bond
  San Diego, CA 92109

Katiunan Chapter
  San Diego City College
  1425 Russ Blvd.
  San Diego, CA 92101

SAN FRANCISCO

J-Town Collective
  1516 A Post
  San Francisco, CA 94109

Everybody's Bookstore
  840 Kearney St.
  San Francisco, CA 94108

I Wor Kuen
  850 Kearney St.
  San Francisco, CA 94108

International Hotel
  848 Kearney St.
  San Francisco, CA 94108

Asian Legal Services
  350 Kearney St.
  San Francisco, CA 94108

Japanese Community Youth Council
  1808 A Sutter St.
  San Francisco, CA 94118

Asian Community Center
  846 Kearney St.
  San Francisco, CA 94108

Kimochi
  22 Peace Plaza
  San Francisco, CA 94115

Chinatown Garment Co-op
  55 ½ Columbus
  San Francisco, CA 94108

Filipino Action Coalition
  311 Minna
  San Francisco, CA 94103

Philippine American Community
Endeavor
    4118 24th St.
    San Francisco, CA 94114

Filipino Coalition of City Coll.of S. F.
    50 Phelan Ave.
    Bungalow B-4
    City College of San Francisco
    San Francisco, CA 94112

Bagong Buhay of City Coll. of S. F.
    City College of San Francisco
    50 Phelan Ave.
    San Francisco, CA 94112

Ating Tao (Pilipino Teatro)
    Oscar Penarando
    422 27th Ave.
    San Francisco, CA 94121

Philippine Club of U. of S. F.
    University of San Francisco
    2130 Fulton
    San Francisco, CA 94117

International Hotel Workers
    832 Kearney St.
    San Francisco, CA 94108

PUBLICATIONS

Rodan
    1808 A Sutter St.
    San Francisco, CA 94115

New Dawn
    P. O. Box 26310
    San Francisco, CA 94126

Kalayan International
    P. O. Box 2919
    San Francisco, CA 94126

Wei Min
    846 Kearney St.
    San Francisco, CA 94108

NORTHERN CALIFORNIA

BERKELEY

East Bay Japanese for Action
    2439 Grove St.
    Berkeley, CA 94704

Asian Communication Project
    509 Eshelman Hall
    UC Berkeley
    Berkeley, CA 94720

Asian Health Caucas
    509 Eshelman Hall
    UC Berkeley
    Berkeley, CA 94720

Filipino American Student Trend of
    S. F. State, UCB, City Coll. of S. F.
    Asian American Studies
    UC Berkeley
    Berkeley, CA 94720

Filipino American Alliance
    UC Berkeley
    Berkeley, CA 94720

OAKLAND

East Bay Chinatown Youth Council
  5527 Shattuck no. 202 or 106
  Oakland, CA 94606

DAVIS

Asian American Studies
  Walker Hall, Room 214
  U.C. Davis
  Davis, CA 95616

STOCKTON

Associated Filipino Youth Organizations
  c/o Luna Jamero
  732-A S. California
  Stockton, CA 95202

Information Referral Center. Pilipino
  c/o Luna Jamero
  732-A South California
  Stockton, CA 95202

Yellow Seed
  728 Barrymore
  Stockton, CA 95204

Asian American Concern
  University of the Pacific
  Stockton, CA 95204

SAN JOSE

Filipino-American Student Association
  San Jose State College
  Washington Square
  San Jose, CA 95114

Asians for Community Action
  565 N. 5th Street
  San Jose, CA 95112

Asian American Studies Office
  San Jose State College
  Barracks No. 9
  195 S. 7th Street
  San Jose, CA 95114

SACRAMENTO

Asian American Legal Services Sacramento
  Asian Community Service Center
  1118 V. Street
  Sacramento, CA

Filipino Community Supporting Change
  Sacramento, CA

People's Bookstore
  2127 10th
  Sacramento, CA 95818

Asian Americans for Action
  ASSSC Sacramento State
  College
  Sacramento, CA 95819

SANTA CRUZ

Asian American Political Alliance
   U. C. Santa Cruz
   c/o Shelley Wong
   6015 Box 150
   Santa Cruz, CA 95060

SALINAS

Filipino Youth of
   Hartnell Community College
   Salinas, CA 93901

HAYWARD

Asian American Cultural Center
   California State College, Hayward
   25400 Hillary Avenue
   Hayward, CA 94542

CUPERTINO

Asian American Studies Program
   De Anza College
   21250 Stevens
   Cupertino, CA 95014

DELANO

Filipino American Political Assoc
   Larry Itliong (Pres.)
   129 West 19th Place
   Delano, CA 93215

Filipino Youth for Community
Development
   c/o Susan Aremas
   1761 East Alisal Street
   Salinas, CA 93901

Asian American Studies Program
   Cal State College at Hayward
   Hayward, CA 95452

STANFORD

AASA
   Stanford University
   552 Alvarado Row
   Stanford, CA 94305

CHICO

Director of Asian and Pacific Studies
   Thomas Johnson
   Dept. of Anthropology
   Chico State College
   Chico, CA 95926

HAWAII

Kahaluu Project
47-536 Kam Highway
Kahaluu, Hawaii, 96734

Ethnic Studies Department
University of Hawaii
Wist Hall 208
1776 University Ave.
Honolulu, Hawaii 96822

PUBLICATIONS

Huli
P.O. Box 963
Kaneohi, Hawaii, 96744

Hawaiian Ethos
P.O. Box 10591
Honolulu, Hawaii, 96816

Paio
P.O. Box 7146
Honolulu, Hawaii, 96821

Hawaii Free People's Press
P.O. Box 10591
Haliewa, Hawaii, 96712

Hawaii Pono Journal
1020 Kuapohahu Dr.
Honolulu, Hawaii 96819

NEW YORK

Asian Women's Coalition
c/o Rose Eng
Barnard College
New York, NY 10027

I Wor Kuen
24 Market St.
New York, NY 10002

The Basement Workshop, Inc.
(Bridge; Yellow Pearl; etc.)
54 Elizabeth St.
New York, NY 10013

Asian Students Organization at
Vassar College   c/o Lesley Yu
Strong 211
Vassar College
Poughkeepsie, NY 12602

Chinese Students Council
c/o Harry Leong
481 McDonald Ave.
Brooklyn, NY 11218

Two Bridges Neighborhood Council
c/o Corky Lee
99 Madison St.
New York, NY 10002

City College of New York
Asian American Studies
Department of Urban and
Ethnic Studies
137 St. and Convent Ave.
New York, NY 10031

Asian Americans for Action
c/o Mary Kochiyama
545 W. 126th St. Apt. 3-B
New York, NY 10027

PUBLICATIONS

Getting Together
  I Wor Kuen
  30 Market St.
  New York, NY 10002

Yellow Pearl
  Basement Workshop
  54 Elizabeth St.
  New York, NY 10013

Harmony; The Writing on the Wall
  c/o Chor Lee
  8320 Bay Parkway
  Brooklyn, NY 11214

EAST COAST

Asian American Student Alliance
  Princeton
  c/o Yang Sheng Liu
  51 Little Hall
  Princeton University
  Princeton, New Jersey 08540

Asian American Student Alliance
  c/o Eric Zen
  Box 2117
  Brown University
  Providence, Rhode Island 02912

Asian American Student Alliance
  Yale
  3374 Yale Station
  New Haven, Conn. 06520

Asian American Student Alliance
  Pennsylvania U.
  c/o Nelson Chan
  East 41 3901 Sprouce
  University of Pennsylvania
  Philadelphia, Penn. 19104

Asian American Law Students
Association
  c/o Nelson Dong; Denis Oyokawa
  2515 Yale Station
  New Haven, Conn. 06520

COLORADO

Asian American EOP
  Elaine Takahashi, Director
  University of Colorado
  Temporary Building 1
  Boulder, Colorado 80302

ARIZONA

People's Center
  412 4th Ave.
  Tucson, Arizona 85705

WASHINGTON

Office of Minority Affairs, Asian Division
  University of Washington
  394 Schmitz
  1400 N.E. Campus Parkway
  Seattle, WA 98105

Filipino Youth Activities of Seattle, Inc.
  507 11th St. Suite 1
  Seattle, WA 98122

Asian Drop-In Center
  2524 Beacon Avenue
  Seattle, Washington 98144

Asian Studies Research Division
  Seattle University
  Seattle, WA 98122

BIBLIOGRAPHY

Boddy, E. Manchester. Japanese In America, Los Angeles: Author, 1921.

Bosworth, Allan R. America's Concentration Camps, New York: W.W. Norton & Co., Inc., 1967.

Commager, Henry Steele, ed. Documents of American History, Vol. II, 8th Ed. New York: Appleton-Century-Crofts, Educational Division, Meredith Corporation, 1971.

Day, A. Grove. Hawaii and Its People. New York: Duell, Sloan and Pearce. 1955.

Dulles, Foster Rhea. Yankees and Samurai - America's Role in the Emergence of Modern Japan: 1791 - 1900. New York: Harper and Row Publishers, Inc., 1965.

Esthus, Raymond A. Theodore Roosevelt and Japan. Seattle: University of Washington Press, 1966.

Hosokawa, Bill. Nisei, The Quiet Americans. New York: William Morrow and Co., Inc., 1969.

Japanese American Curriculum Project. Japanese Americans - The Untold Story. New York: Holt, Rinehart and Winston, Inc., 1971.

Kitano, Harry H. L., Japanese Americans - The Evolution of a Subculture, Englewood Cliffs, N.J.: Prentice-Hall, Inc., 1969.

McWilliams, Carey. Prejudice - Japanese Americans: Symbol of Racial Intolerance. Boston: Little, Brown and Co., 1944.

Myer, Dillon S. Uprooted Americans: Japanese Americans and the War Relocation Authority During World War II. Tucson: University of Arizona Press, 1971.

Petersen, William L. Japanese Americans. Oppression and Success, Ethnic Groups in Comparative Perspective, Random House Series. New York: Random House, Inc., 1971.

Reischauer, Edwin O. The United States and Japan. Cambridge, Mass.: Harvard University Press, 1950.

COMPILATION OF OTHER BIBLIOGRAPHY

Asian Americans: An Annotated Bibliography. UCLA Asian American
    Studies Center: 1971.

Asians in America. University of California - Davis, Asian American
    Research Project: 1970.

Estes, Don, comp. Selected Bibliography on the Japanese American Ex-
    perience. San Francisco: JACL, National Headquarters, 1972.